A
Year
of
Birdsong

First published in the United Kingdom in 2022 by
B.T. Batsford
43 Great Ormond Street
London WC1N 3HZ

An imprint of B.T. Batsford Holdings Ltd

ISBN: 9781849947305

A CIP catalogue record for this book is available from the
British Library.

10 9 8 7 6 5 4 3 2 1

Reproduction by Rival Colour Ltd, UK
Printed and bound by Toppan Leefung Ltd, China

This book can be ordered direct from the publisher at
www.batsfordbooks.com, or try your local bookshop.

MIX
Paper from
responsible sources
FSC® C104723
www.fsc.org

A
Year
of
Birdsong

Dominic Couzens
ILLUSTRATED BY Madeleine Floyd

BATSFORD

Contents

Introduction

BIRDSONG IS ONE OF THE JOYS OF LIFE FOR THOSE OF us fortunate enough to be able to hear it. It is also a free gift, requiring no charge to appreciate, although recognizing the species might require the help of a tutor or an app. This gift is offered all around the world. Other than some inhospitable desert and polar regions, and over the open ocean, the sound is everywhere, even in the midst of urban centres. And it is almost universally adored. You rarely hear people saying: 'I hate the sound of birds singing,' unless their sleep has been broken at dawn, in which case the birds themselves are quickly forgiven.

The universality of birdsong also extends to the year. While in many parts of the world the zenith of the phenomenon, and the high tide of the dawn chorus, is seasonal, that doesn't mean that it ceases completely. There are always wild voices out there, even lone ones. A drop in singing in one part of the globe might well coincide with a swelling in another, so while the northern hemisphere birds go quiet in summer and autumn, their counterparts in the southern hemisphere start to warm up. In the tropics the best bird choruses coincide with rainy seasons, when most birds are breeding. So, within these pages we can enjoy an authentic year of birdsong around the world.

This book celebrates 52 memorable bird songs, one for each week of the year. The species and their noises are chosen for many different reasons; not all of the featured voices are even particularly harmonious. Some are chosen because they are apposite to the season, others because they demonstrate an interesting piece of bird song research. Some songs reflect on us, and how we hear and appreciate them. There are stories associated with songs, and literary masterpieces inspired by them. Some songs have an irresistible sense of place.

Although there are birds featured from all over the world, I have chosen mostly from species that are well-known to audiences in Europe and North America. One reason is purely commercial; there might be some wonderful songs from Madagascar, for example, but readers are going to prefer to read about sounds that they know or can imagine hearing. However, the other reason is that most bird song research has been done in these parts of the world, so the most interesting stories and insights, at least until recently, tended to come from here.

The book has been specially written so that any reader can at least get some idea of the actual sound of the bird from a description in words, or even a memory phrase used to identify it. It could be read cover to cover without hearing any of the voices within. However, there is no substitute for actually hearing the songs and calls described, so we have included QR codes. I suggest that you also use a birdsong app (such as Merlin, which covers much of the world) or visit a website such as Xeno-Canto. Many of the songs are on YouTube as well. Most are easy to find online.

Before you read the accounts that follow, it is necessary for me to explain a few very important terms that are used throughout the book, and also to give a brief explanation of what bird vocalizations are actually for. Without these explanations, certain pages might cause puzzlement.

The book is entitled *A Year of Birdsong*, but not all the sounds featured are, strictly speaking, songs. That's because birders make a (rather loose) distinction between songs and calls. Part of this distinction is purely descriptive, but a significant amount lies in the biological purpose of the vocalization.

To those of us hearing them, bird SONGS are typically complex vocalizations that last a few seconds at least. They are multisyllabic, and could perhaps be described as sentences, or even paragraphs, depending on the bird. On the other hand, those same species might make different, usually less elaborate vocalizations, which are single words or syllables, or sometimes trills and screams. These are CALLS, or CALL NOTES, which are part of the simpler vocabulary of the bird.

Bird songs are usually seasonal. These more intricate vocalizations rise and fall with the breeding season. In many species, at least part of the song is learned. In the majority of species, especially in temperate parts of the world, they are sung largely, or even only by males. The function of a song is primarily twofold. The male is the main claimer and keeper of a territory, so it sings to other males to keep them away. However, the same (or a different) song is also directed at females, with the intention of attracting their attention and, in a perfect world, eventually mating with them. There are many variations of this theme but understanding its fundamentals will help.

Although most birds, especially those that live in forests or scrubland, sing their songs from a perch, a significant minority perform from the ground, or up in the air, while flying. For the sake of definition, songs which are uttered wholly or usually in flight are known as 'flight songs', and the displays in which songs are uttered are known as 'song flights'.

Calls are used in many contexts and can be very specific, such as those used to incite copulation, or have a broader purpose, such as alarm. They aren't usually learned, but innate.

The situation is complicated by birds that aren't strictly songbirds making sounds that are, effectively, a song! Let me explain. Birds are divided into many different groups, by far the largest of which is known as passerines. It's an unequal divide: more than 60 per cent of the world's species are sparrow-like passerines, including many of the ones we know best, such as warblers, finches, tits, thrushes and swallows. These passerines are often called perching birds on account of their opposing toe arrangement on the foot, with three facing forwards and one back, allowing for an excellent perching grip. However, passerines are also the world's main songbirds. This is due to the nature of their sound-producing organ, the syrinx, situated at the bottom of the windpipe, where it divides into the two bronchi (branches) of the lungs. It is much more complicated and advanced than those of other birds – with extra rings, musculature, and so on. The passerine syrinx is a marvel, and much of what makes them special.

However, the lack of a fancy syrinx does not exclude non-passerine birds from defending their territory or attracting a mate by vocalizing. Birds such as cuckoos and doves, for example, obviously do this, often loudly and atmospherically. But they inherit their 'songs', and although their voices are often individually distinct and recognizable, they don't add to them by learning. On the whole, I have tried to call the sounds that they make ADVERTISING CALLS.

There is one more technical matter to describe. Bird song is complex, especially when you listen carefully, and it sometimes needs to be broken down into its constituent parts. For example, birds might repeat a sentence again and again – this is best described as a PHRASE. Within a phrase (or a long monologue) there are often easily distinguished sections, some with several or multiple syllables. These can be called ELEMENTS or STROPHES, the ingredients of the song.

Finally, I will briefly mention a bird sound that is very famous but is not included as itself in the book, and that is the DAWN CHORUS. Clearly, it's a jumble of voices, but not of a single species. Nevertheless, it is a theme throughout the book. Despite the fact that it occurs around the world, and has drawn much attention, it is poorly understood. Why should birds start singing in the predawn darkness?

There are various hypotheses. Firstly, the transmission of song is often enhanced at dawn, either by atmospheric conditions or the sheer lack of other competing sounds, including human ones. Secondly, dawn song is relatively safe, because night predators are thinking of retiring and the day predators will wait for the light. And thirdly, it's too dark to find food during the predawn, so it won't interfere with other activities.

However, these hypotheses cannot explain the full phenomenon, because none of them compel a bird to sing; they just facilitate it. The dawn chorus surely has a compulsion element. One is that, after the night, a bird is wise to protect its territory and mate by reminding everybody that it is still there. Vacancies are noticed immediately and borders soon broken when not defended.

And then there is the effect on the female. The dawn chorus is often at its height, in a particular species, during egg laying, when the female is most fertile; it also peaks at dawn, when a bird has just laid an egg. During this time the male must be vigilant, noisy and impossible for the female to ignore. A male that isn't singing loudly close by the nest before dawn is likely to find that its mate's attention wanders elsewhere. A male's fear of losing its paternity is not the most joyful explanation for the dawn chorus, but it is certainly intriguing!

And song is intriguing. And beautiful, and wonderful; and it lifts the heart. My hope is that, in a small way, this book will do the same.

Rifleman

Acanthisitta chloris

NEW ZEALAND, 7–9 cm (2¾–3½ in)

IN A BOOK ON SONGBIRDS IT MIGHT SEEM odd to begin with a bird that barely has a song at all. Shouldn't we start with a bang, a clash of cymbals to lift off the year, or introduce the subject with a soaring, glorious voice that will elevate every heart? What's the point in listening to the squeak of a rifleman, a midget that lives in the lush southern beech forests of New Zealand? It utters merely a high-pitched 'seep' sound, which many people can only hear if they strain their ears.

Why indeed? Well, great things have a habit of starting small and quietly. The best New Year resolutions aren't the loud promises we make to others, but the silent hopes that are barely whispered.

If you watch the rifleman foraging and calling on a chilly morning on an alpine slope in New Zealand, you might see a diminutive bird, but what you hear is a voice from deep time. Those quiet trills are stirrings. They are close to what was probably the first sound made by any songbird anywhere on Earth, a breath taken as the non-avian dinosaurs breathed their last.

The rifleman is a member of the most ancient living group of songbirds – or at least the most ancient group known from the original songbird lineage, which evolved around 60 million years ago. The rifleman's family, or New Zealand wrens, are known to have evolved about 55 million years ago, when they branched off from those ancestral forebears. The New Zealand wrens have the simplest sound producing organ, the syrinx, of any songbirds, without any intrinsic muscles, and confined to the trachea. Within the body of the tiny rifleman, and reflected in its breath, is the origin of all the finest bird songs we hear today.

They are close to what was probably the first sound made by any songbird anywhere on earth, a breath taken as the non-avian dinosaurs breathed their last.

Not long ago, scientists assumed that the passerines must have evolved somewhere in the northern hemisphere. However, through DNA sequencing studies and by looking at the palaeogeography of the shifting continents, it is now known this isn't so. Surprising as it may seem, bird song as we know it began in that part of Gondwanaland that is now Australasia.

That means that every one of our northern hemisphere favourites – larks and warblers, thrushes and nightingales, wrens and mockingbirds, robins and robin-chats, babblers, tits and finches – owes their song prowess to birds that first opened their mouths in that southern region. The dawn chorus, the melodrama of spring, the territorial song flights, the duets, the major soundtrack of the wild – it all began down under.

Bird song as we know it began in that part of Gondwanaland that is now Australasia.

And, of course, so does our year. The first day of January begins in Oceania and spins westwards. New Zealand is one of the first places to receive the New Year sunlight. And the chances are that, for countless millennia, the quiet calls of the rifleman were among the first species to cast their sounds to the air every year. Small beginnings indeed.

Song thrush

Turdus philomelos

WESTERN EUROPE; FURTHER EAST TO CENTRAL ASIA,
20–25 cm (8–9 in)

IT HAPPENS NOW UNTIL APRIL AT LEAST, without fail. Every year is the same. The gardens of Britain and Northern Europe resound to a sweet-voiced bird song, and everybody is confused.

'I've heard this loud song in my garden,' says a neighbour. 'Can you tell me what it might be?' Another says: 'I keep getting woken up by this bird singing in the dark and I've tried all the bird apps, and still don't know what it is.' The answer is always the same. It's a song thrush. It really is, honestly.

The reason why it confuses people is that listeners just hear a few fragments of a seemingly distinctive song and think it should be obvious what it is. But this is a classic case of information impatience. If everybody just gave the bird a chance to show off its regular singing rhythm, they would find it easy to identify. You just have to give it time.

The song of the song thrush has been described thus in a guidebook: 'Loud, varied and with a distinct tendency for rhythmic repetition of phrases.' But far better, and soaked with artistic glamour, are these lines from the poem 'Home Thoughts from Abroad', written by English romantic poet Robert Browning in 1845:

That's the wise thrush; he sings each song twice over,
Lest you should think he never could recapture
The first fine careless rapture!

The essence of this thrush, then, is that it repeats every phrase (or strophe) several times, in a studied, unhurried fashion. It then moves on to another phrase and repeats that, too, and the next. So you will hear something like: 'It's me, it's me, it's me! I'm a song thrush, I'm a song thrush, I'm a song thrush! Listen out, listen out! I'm here, I'm here, I'm here, I'm here ...'. In all, a single song thrush may have more than 200 phrases in its vocabulary, although it will tend to use favourites again and again.

The other characteristics of the song are that it is loud, clear and well-enunciated – all of which means that it's very easy to notice, breaking out from the running soundtrack of your everyday mind, even when you aren't a frequent listener to bird song.

The song thrush's proclamations are a serenade of earliness, both of the year and the day.

Another reason for those January bird song enquiries is that the song thrush's proclamations are a serenade of earliness, both of the year and the day. It sings at its best during the lightening or the darkening of the sky. It is naturally a bird that feeds in shade, so the predawn and dusk are its comfort zones. In these conditions it is often a lone voice or is sharing the airwaves with the European robin (see page 156); but it can easily be dominant, so if a sleepy person is opening the curtains or leaving home for the day shift, this is the song that they hear.

There are several intriguing peculiarities about the song thrush and its song. It can start singing as early as November, a couple of months before many resident birds, presumably to establish a territory for the future breeding season. Its peak starts early. Most unusually for any bird, the song thrush also appears to have no visual displays to begin or cement the pair bond. The song is evidently the key. Again unusually, the male stops singing, except at dawn and dusk, as soon as it is paired. Yet another curious behaviour is that in midsummer there is another late resurgence of song, perhaps when young birds can try out their own voices for the first time (see chaffinch, page 28).

It seems as though even when you know the singer is a song thrush, not all your questions are easily answered.

Great horned owl

Bubo virginianus

NORTH AMERICA AND SOUTH AMERICA
(OUTSIDE AMAZONIA), 46–63 cm (18–24 in)

THE NORTHERN FORESTS ARE IN THE GRIP of winter; nights are desperately cold and seemingly never-ending. The very idea of thriving, let alone surviving, in such conditions would seem almost impossible. But for the great horned owl, that mighty owl of all the Americas, the breeding season is about to begin, even in regions fringing the Arctic.

All through the longest nights, this owl has been sending out its solemn, foghorn-like advertising call, which echoes through forests on still, frosty nights, carrying far. The male doesn't mince its hoots – one rendition of the five-syllable phrase could be 'Who ... the hell ... are ... you?' It doesn't sound friendly, and it isn't meant to be; great horned owls are fiercely territorial and will kill persistent intruders.

But the doleful hooting has another purpose, exemplified by the fact that the female great horned owl duets with its mate at this time of the year. Although the female is larger than the male, its voice is higher pitched, and it characteristically adds a few more hoots to its feminine phrase. The male typically starts a bout of duetting, then the female calls, then the male again, and so on; and both sexes sometimes start before the other one has finished. Duetting is, of course, about togetherness. Great horned owls make long-term, and probably lifelong, pair bonds, cocooned in their exclusive territory.

Duetting is, of course, about togetherness. Great horned owls make long-term, and probably lifelong, pair bonds, cocooned in their exclusive territory.

Remarkably, then, now in late January, the female may lay its first egg, although this can happen any time between now and mid-March. The birds are thought to start this early so that the young hatch with enough time to learn hunting skills before next winter kicks in. Even so, conditions can be tough; great horned owls have been found incubating eggs in external temperatures of -30 °C (-22 °F).

The great horned owl's hunting skills are remarkable. It sits on an elevated perch in the darkness and waits for something to move below, whereupon it will drop on its target, killing the animal with its talons. These owls take a wide range of prey, mainly mammals, from small rodents to rabbits and hares, as well as birds of all sizes – legend has it that they will kill turkeys. They are famed, of course, for their remarkable vision and hearing, the former being at least three times better than our night vision (which is actually quite good by most standards). Their eyes are packed with super-sensitive rod cells, ideal for contrast in low lighting conditions. Their hearing is undoubtedly superior to ours, the owl depending on its ability to make out the slightest rustle below, which might betray a prey animal. It is a curiosity that a great horned own listens for high-pitched cues such as squeaks and crackles, yet its owl calls are invariably deep. Perhaps the difference is intentional.

The nocturnal habits of owls have long fed the notion that these birds are somehow mysterious, untrustworthy; creatures to be feared. In some parts of the world, they are considered to be spirits and devils, taboo, well worth avoiding. For many years the Apache peoples of North America kept up the tradition of burning down the houses of the departed, so that owls could take their spirits away. It is a deep part of our humanity to fear the dark, so it isn't surprising that those who inhabit the night should be in league with the shadows.

And yet the magnificent hoot of the great horned owl, calling in the depths of the late winter night, is something very different. It is surely a calling of life, a hastening of the end of the cold. We all delight in those early spring birds, the American robins (see page 44) on one side of the Atlantic and blackbirds (page 32) on the other. The shrill vibrancy speaks the promise of spring. Yet the hoots of owls make the same promise earlier. The message might seem sterner, but it is no less optimistic.

Greater hoopoe-lark

Alaemon alaudipes

NORTH AFRICA; FURTHER EAST TO PAKISTAN
AND INDIA, 19–25 cm (7½–9 in)

 IF YOU WERE EVER TO SEEK A LIST OF the world's best bird songs online, you might be surprised to learn that the greater hoopoe-lark is often included among the usual icons such as nightingales and mockingbirds. The hoopoe-lark is a pretty obscure species found in the deserts of North Africa and the Middle East, and further eastwards to the arid areas of Pakistan. Not many people are fortunate enough ever to hear one in person.

There is, of course, a whiff of the romantic about selecting a poorly known bird to appear along with the megastars; the amateur acting alongside Hollywood giants. But there is, of course, no reason to leave out an obscure bird either.

The greater hoopoe-lark certainly has a distinctive and unusual song. There is a series of slow, flutey whistles that aren't far off pure tones, together with some imaginative trills. It is definitely a song to make you sit up and listen; few birds in the world sound like it.

But is it one of the best? Nobody could ever say definitively. It is a matter of taste.

However, as one who has had the privilege of hearing this bird in the wild, I can unequivocally say that it is one of my favourites. And that isn't only because of the song itself. It is because of the context. Few bird songs sit so perfectly in the place where they are heard.

The hoopoe-lark is a bird of desolate habitats, where the lack of water turns the landscape into shades of pastels. Wherever you see it, there are long views around you, uninterrupted, and big skies above. The lark occurs both in rocky places and on the sand, usually where bushes are sparse and often spiny. It is a ferocious environment with a brutal simplicity. Somehow it would be entirely wrong to utter an upbeat, fulsome ditty here. This is a stage for the plaintive, the mellow and the melancholic.

To appreciate a hoopoe-lark at its best, you also need to be there beside it at daybreak, when its song is most vigorous. And as everybody knows, deserts are extreme. In many of this lark's favoured locations, the cold bites in the morning. But the sheer discomfort adds to the adventure of hearing one. During the summer, hoopoe-larks retreat into the unused burrows of rodents. There they remain for hours, 20–30cm (8–12in) underground, until the cool of the evening. Theirs is a twilight existence.

But the ultimate reason why the hoopoe-lark's song is such an experience to savour is that the bird choreographs a 'sky dance' to enhance it!

The bird sings its slow, melodious, piping phrases, adds in a quick trill and then launches into the air, usually from the top of a bush. At this moment it transforms from a medium-sized, soberly plumaged bird into a much more striking self, showing off its bold black-and-white wings (which explain the name, as the wing pattern and overall shape are similar to the Eurasian hoopoe *Upupa epops*). Once again uttering its needle-sharp, plaintive notes, it now rises up to anywhere between a couple of metres and 25m (6½–82ft) above the ground. In the cold, fresh air it suddenly appears to lose all control, stalling and rolling, and very quickly plummeting to the ground head-first. Only at the last minute does this show-off pull out of its dive and flutter back to the perch from whence it came. Set against the backdrop of the stark but lovely desert landscape, this is a truly spectacular show of acrobatics and star-quality singing.

The bird sings its slow, melodious, piping phrases, adds in a quick trill and then launches into the air, usually from the top of a bush.

It is this combination that makes the hoopoe-lark such a compelling performer. It is the place, the time of day, the haunting melody and the visual show that transform a very good bird song into something truly special.

Common chaffinch

Fringilla coelebs

EUROPE AND WESTERN ASIA, 14–18 cm (5½–7 in)

IN THE STILL-LEAFLESS WOODS OF EUROPE and western Asia, one of the most abundant birds has just begun to sing. It's February, the traditional time for the spring to liven up to the sound of chaffinches, whose simple rattling phrases will soon echo across almost every woodland glade. What many people don't realize, however, is that most of those chaffinches will be singing badly.

The idea of a bird performing poorly – when that bird could be a nightingale or other similar icon that sears the soul – is hardly believable to many. But that is to misunderstand what bird song is, and how it arises.

The fact is that, about now, many of Europe's chaffinches are making a complete mess of what should be a simple task. Their song is simple, merely a short and agreeably cheerful phrase that accelerates to a flourish at the end. For those fans of cricket, the phrase has been likened to the sound of a slow bowler's quickening footsteps as they approach the crease, with the flourish upon delivering the ball. However you might describe it, the chaffinch's straightforward efforts make it one of the most easily recognizable of bird songs.

However, if you listen carefully at the moment, you might be underwhelmed. Where there should be structure in the chaffinch's song, there is mush; and where there should be a zenith, there is zilch. Is there such a thing as a half-rattle? If so, it describes the feeble efforts well.

Half-rattles they might be, but these efforts are not half-hearted; in fact, they are earnest. The reason why chaffinches may sound a little rusty on these late winter mornings is that the singers – all males not yet a year old – are practising.

It is easy to think that a bird is born with a complete and finished song in its brain. That is indeed the case for many bird species. But in the more advanced songbirds – those with particularly complicated voice-producing apparatus – there is much more exciting room for variety. A great many of our songbirds learn their songs.

To be honest, the chaffinch is not one of the world's greatest and most creative songbirds. But scientists have studied it carefully and have uncovered some remarkable facts about how a chaffinch acquires its song. And the half-baked songs of February are part of that picture.

The chaffinch is indeed born with a song in its brain, but it is only a template, not the complete finished product. The template ensures that a chaffinch doesn't suddenly sing like a greenfinch or a robin or a blackbird; if such a thing happened, the intended audience – other chaffinches – would be deaf to its charms. To hold territory, or to acquire a mate, a chaffinch must sound like a chaffinch. But the template is only that – the framework for something altogether more interesting.

During a young chaffinch's first few months, its 'sensitive period', it listens to the voices around it. The primary voice, its main tutor you might say, is likely to be its own father, but there will be input from the neighbours as well – and they will not necessarily sound exactly the same. The youngster absorbs the chaffinch-specific soundscape of its youth. The seed is sown during the breeding season from which it spawned. When that breeding season passes, and the youngster moults its plumage and may migrate away, there is a silent period when nothing much happens to its song output.

In early spring, however, as the days lengthen and testosterone surges in its body, the young bird, back on the breeding grounds, is compelled to sing. It puts into practice what it has learned. Not only will it hear other adults start to sing, but it will also hear the sound of its own voice for the first time. Now is the crucial point when, it terms of its song output, it comes of age.

The half-rattles don't last long and what emerges instead is full chaffinch song, flourish and all. The youngster puts meat on its template – its father's songs, its neighbours' songs, and potentially the odd flight of fancy of its own. In a few weeks the newcomer is in possession of something special – its own very personal singing repertoire. There are infinite variations possible within its song structure, and these come to the fore.

The chaffinch could use the ultimate, unvarying stereotyped song, producing no more than a template. But allowing for learning lets loose the wondrous possibilities of individuality. In theory, any bird could invent sounds that have never been sung by its species before. In a few short weeks, something special could arise in those leafy branches.

Eurasian blackbird

Turdus merula

EUROPE AND WESTERN ASIA, 24–27 cm (9½–10½ in)

IT'S MID-FEBRUARY, AND IN BRITAIN AND Europe winter doesn't yet know it's beaten. But the blackbirds have started singing, firing their golden rays of vocal warmth at its icy grip, loosening the cruel fingers of frost little by little, phrase by phrase. It won't be long before winter retreats and blackbird song holds sway.

The emergence of blackbird song arguably ends the overture of early spring. There have been snatches before, but now the dawn chorus and the daytime babble take on a new strength and quality. With due respect to the song thrush, there is a harmonious strength added by the blackbird, a transcendent polish that grips the listener in an entirely new way.

For me, the blackbird song nourishes my soul more than any other. It isn't because it is a fine melody, although it certainly is –

the song consists of glorious, mellow fluting phases that are each quite short, each different, and each delivered after a respectful pause. It isn't because of the blackbird's effortless virtuosity, much as it is stirring to hear anything at the top of its game. For me, the blackbird is a statement against hurry in an accelerating world. It is a reassuring reminder that everything is in its place. It is a song that oozes calm, whatever life's backdrop might be.

The song consists of glorious, mellow fluting phases that are each quite short, each different, and each delivered after a respectful pause.

In recent years, bird songs – at least the melodious ones, such as the blackbird's – have attracted interest in how they can potentially enhance mental health. There is now some impressive evidence that being in nature and hearing wild sounds helps us to refocus and feel better. Studies from King's College, London, show that listening to five minutes of bird song a day can lower your blood pressure and calm you down; apparently, this effect can last up to four hours. Ongoing research at the University of Surrey, in the UK, showed that certain species make some people feel happier and more relaxed – the best songs are gentler, higher-pitched and complex. On a more general level, a survey by Natural England in the UK (Monitoring Engagement with the Natural Environment), with 500,000 respondents, showed that 90 per cent of people felt refreshed and invigorated by being outside, and that people who visited the natural environment most often have the greatest life satisfaction, more self-worth, greater happiness and less anxiety. Being in nature also leads to better overall health. Although in their infancy, these are pretty astonishing results.

But why should we feel better in the company of nature? It is thought that being in nature takes us back to where we belong – essentially, humans have been living in the wild for most of their evolutionary history, and towns and cities are so far removed from this that it causes us stress. Bird songs are an indication that a place is rich in resources, and these automatically make us feel safer.

Another theory is that being in nature helps us bring order to the thought processes in our brain. A noisy environment, such as a workplace, busy commute or a home with children, can have the effect of scrambling our brains, and time in nature can help us untangle them. Imagine, after a hectic day, how a dose of blackbird song could simply make those layers of stress fall away. You could call it 'birdfulness'.

Of course, at this time of the year, the swelling bird chorus – at least now in the northern hemisphere – is giving us a clear message of hope. It is saying that longer days and summer heaven is completely guaranteed in the near future. February is spring's 'secret is out' month, when the signs are too great to ignore. We know it is coming.

That message of spring hope, wherever it is in the world, has always offered a future of good things. Now, with many of us living in the abundant, well-stocked developed world, we might appreciate the extra warmth and colour. For our ancestors living off the land, and for the many who still depend on the land for food, it guaranteed more food in the belly, greater variety and resources. Perhaps more than anything, though, the swelling bird song promised a reduction of fear. Food and life would soon become more dependable and certain as the spring and summer took hold.

If bird songs help reduce the deep emotion of fear, it is no surprise that they makes us feel better. Go out, listen, and revel in them.

White-throated sparrow

Zonotrichia albicollis

NORTH AMERICA, 16 cm (6½ in)

THE SONG OF THE WHITE-THROATED sparrow is frost in note form. This northern waif, abundant all over the taiga forests of North America, is the sprite of the wilderness, its whistling notes echoing from the tops of evergreens. Its phrase is the spring snowfall and the swollen, rushing river, but it also forms the backdrop to longer days and emerging mosquitoes. It is crisp, pure and needle-sharp.

Emerging birders love it, too. Is there any bird song in the continent that is easier to hear and identify? For years, people have expressed it in phrases: 'Old ... Sam ... Peabody, Peabody, Peabody', or perhaps more appropriately given its breeding range: 'Oh ... sweet ... Canada, Canada, Canada'. The song is relatively loud and simple, with only small changes in pitch, and each male sings just one song, so there's very little variety to get confused about. There really is nothing like it. Once you've mastered the white-throated sparrow, you can conquer the rest.

It isn't only novice bird-song learners that love white-throated sparrows. Scientists do, too. This species shows several very intriguing characteristics that are unusual among birds, of which the most obvious, and oddest, is that this species comes in two forms.

This northern waif, abundant all over the taiga forests of North America, is the sprite of the wilderness, its whistling notes echoing from the tops of evergreens.

Study white-throated sparrows carefully and you might notice that some look smarter than others and their head markings are slightly different. The smart birds are endowed with neat smoky-grey breasts and head sides, and the white on the throat and especially the stripe over the eye (supercilium) is as bright as snow. Their fellow sparrows, however, aren't as pure grey, are streakier and, fundamentally, their supercilium is not white but a dull tan colour. These are not male and female, but the two forms, white-striped and tan-striped, which occur in both sexes.

What is very strange is that the two forms show different behaviour patterns. For example, the smart white-striped forms are more aggressive and much more likely to attempt to mate with a member of the opposite sex to which they are not formally paired. The tan-striped forms, on the other hand, are better parents, providing more care to their young. White-stripes show higher testosterone levels.

The distinctions also extend to their singing behaviour. White-striped males sing a great deal more than tan-striped males; and while tan-striped females hardly ever sing, their white-striped counterparts do.

Now, you might think that the white-stripes would be more successful than the tan-stripes and cause their rivals to suffer. However, this doesn't happen, because when it comes to pairing up, the opposites attract. It turns out that white-stripes almost always pair up with tan-stripes. Scientists have a wonderful term to describe this type of pairing, which keeps both forms in existence – disassortative mating.

Another fascinating quirk of white-throated sparrow biology is that its song seems to be changing. Earlier I mentioned how people would use the 'Old ... Sam ... Peabody, Peabody, Peabody' phrase to identify this bird. This phrase was ubiquitous until about the 1960s, but since then it has slowly begun to die out. The three-note 'Peabody' has become two notes, sounding more like 'cherry'. Strangely, it seems that all the birds throughout the continent have shortened their songs. It is surely coincidence that this has happened just as human attention spans have waned.

Great spotted woodpecker

Dendrocopos major

EURASIA EAST TO JAPAN, 20–24 cm (8–9½ in)

IF BIRDS' VOICES MELD TO CREATE A WILD symphony, then woodpeckers form the percussion section. While many songbirds sound sweet and tuneful to our ears, the loud drumming of woodpeckers, a worldwide 'rat-a-tat', is a different beast – definitely a rhythm, not a melody. People everywhere recognize that the familiar drum-beat comes from hitting wood with its beak, which is, of course, what woodpeckers do for a living.

The woodpecker's drum is misunderstood, though. Many people think that the rapid striking is made when the bird is excavating a hole, but this isn't the case. The bird taps the wood, not to make a hole but to send a message. That's not to say that woodpeckers don't make any sound as they batter wood to create a hole for a nest, or to expose juicy grubs hidden in the bark. They make a pecking noise then, too, but it is irregular and fitful. Their working beats are slow, deliberate and destructive, rather like the heavy, hefty beats of human road workers breaking through tarmac with a pickaxe.

But the woodpecker's drumming is equivalent to a musician beating a drum, hitting its surface without damaging it. Likewise, the woodpecker doesn't breach the resonant branch of dead wood that it uses for its drumming performance. It is non-destructive, but sonorous.

If you live in the northern hemisphere, you might have noticed something else about the woodpecker's drum: it is seasonal. It reaches its zenith about now, in the early part of the breeding season. In spring a great spotted woodpecker may drum 200 times a day, and three times that if it hasn't yet secured a mate. By June, however, the drumming declines and by the autumn the ringing wood resonates no more.

And that's because the woodpecker's drum takes the place of a song and performs the same functions. How does the woodpecker defend and proclaim its territory? By drumming. How does a woodpecker make its presence known to a potential mate? It drums – and males and females drum in slightly different ways, although how exactly depends on the species of woodpecker. In the case of the great spotted woodpecker, the female tends to give shorter series of drums, which can allow male and female not just to meet and mate but to coordinate their breeding rhythms. They even drum together when checking out holes for a potential nest. It's a convenient way to communicate, because the noise is particularly far-carrying through the woods and forests where the birds live.

The sheer speed at which a woodpecker can tap wood is remarkable. The great spotted woodpecker, for example, makes an average of 13 strikes in just over half a second. This species is distinguished by the attack at the beginning of its drum and then the very quick fade at the end. The lesser spotted woodpecker, which occurs in many of the same parts of the world, has a longer-lasting drum that doesn't fade at all but carries on like a power drill. On occasion, though, woodpeckers seem to get confused or overstimulated, and the two species can be heard duetting together.

Drumming makes sense for woodpeckers, of course, and it stands to reason that they should use it for communication. After all, many species spend much of their day battering their bills against wood, so from there it is an easy step to their treetop form of Morse code.

The sheer speed at which a woodpecker can tap wood is remarkable. The great spotted woodpecker, for example, makes an average of 13 strikes in just over half a second.

American robin

Turdus migratorius

NORTH AMERICA, 25 cm (AROUND 10 in)

'CHEER UP, CHEER UP ...' IT SEEMS TO SAY. And, let's face it, we all need cheering up. No wonder the American robin is that continent's favourite singer. Its message isn't complicated, and few would ever describe its song as fantastic, or the singer as a virtuoso. But who cares? It has found its way into people's hearts – and for a good many reasons.

This ruddy-breasted thrush could be described as the all-American bird. Its range stretches from east to west and from California and Texas north into the Arctic Circle. It is as familiar in the vast northern taiga forests as it is along streams in the Midwest and in gardens of the Gulf Coast. Not only does it sing from treetops overlooking glades where no human has ever wandered, it also sings in urban plots in densely populated cities. The song may compete with roaring traffic and sirens in New York, while elsewhere it may complement the early evening howling of a wolf pack in Alaska. This is Every-bird, the constant companion, the unifier, the cheerer-up.

To many ears, it is also the bringer of spring. American robins start singing early, in late winter, when warm weather is just a thought, not a reality. We humans love to anticipate good things. A robin singing on a bright, breezy March day with snow on the ground lifts our hearts – 'Cheer up, cheer up ...'. The same robin sings all day in May and June, and makes much less impact, but its work is already done.

The song may compete with roaring traffic and sirens in New York, while elsewhere it may complement the early evening howling of a wolf pack in Alaska.

The song in isolation is hardly a marvel. There might be ten or more 'Cheer up' phrases, with some 'cheerily' mixed in, and a distinctive rising and falling in pitch. The phrases are loud and piercing, which gives the song its edge. The average robin has about 10–20 different phrases in its repertoire, although these are hard to distinguish without careful listening. But even this level of variety does not make the song exceptional.

What is unusual, though, is the sheer effort the bird puts in. It is often the first soloist to be heard in the morning chorus (some birds may start at 3 a.m. in temperate America in spring) and, in particular, it is the last voice left standing at night, when it might have the twilight all to itself. Up in the far north, where the light is almost endless in summer, so is the chorus of American robins. The concert might go on, quite literally, for hours. The bird is accustomed to twilight. Its eyes are unusually large for the size of bird, and in its non-singing day job it hunts in the leaf-litter in deep shade.

Listen carefully enough to an American robin and you might hear some slightly different sounds. Among all the 'Cheer ups' and their subtle variations, such as 'Cheerios' – the so-called carolling phrases – there might be some more

It is often the first soloist to be heard in the morning chorus and it is the last voice left standing at night.

mysterious notes, sounding perhaps like 'Hisselly', with a quality quite apart from the rest. Remarkably, each robin may have 75–100 different 'Hisselly' phrases in its song, but so far scientists haven't discovered their purpose.

To most of us, this doesn't matter. To most of us, all we need is a tonic poured down from the treetops.

Reed bunting

Emberiza schoeniclus

EURASIA EAST TO JAPAN, 14–16 cm (5½–6½ in)

THE REED BUNTING'S SONG IS NOBODY'S favourite, absent from everybody's playlists. After a day's springtime birdwatching in Britain or Europe, people never say: 'It was just so marvellous to hear those beautiful reed buntings singing.' The song has been described in at least one guidebook as 'Monotonously repeated ... disjointed, short, simple, slow ...'. At the very best it's an album filler, a piece of natural muzak that you wouldn't choose to buy.

It does have the value of being distinctive, though, which is good news for those same birdwatchers. Slow and staccato, the song could be transcribed as 'Three ... blind ... mice'. Another clever description is that the reed bunting 'sounds like a human toddler learning to count but forgetting what happens after three'. We should perhaps be grateful it isn't yet another incomprehensible bird song.

What's it doing in this book, then? Is there anything special about it? You bet. Few other birds in the world give away their status and motivations so easily. It's all about the speed of the song and the number of notes. If you can work this out, you have a window into the life of a wild bird.

Believe it or not, a reed bunting's song betrays its marital status. If the song has just three notes, delivered quite slowly and falteringly, and fitting the 'Three blind mice' description, your bird is paired up. If the song has more notes – perhaps five or six – delivered in the same time period but more quickly, it is unpaired. When a male is singing the 'slow song' (paired), it leaves quite short intervals between songs. If it is singing the 'fast song', it leaves a longer interval between songs. A male that loses its mate during the March breeding season switches from a slow song back to a fast song, so there's no doubt that the song is an admission of its life situation. But there's more.

In 2009 a study in Sweden discovered something astonishing. They realized that, overlooked for a hundred years, the reed bunting doesn't just have two songs – it has three. To unmask something so significant in a common and well-studied bird doesn't happen very often. They worked out that the reed bunting has a special dawn song, which is like a continuous stream of phrases with short intervals between them – similar to a fast song uttered without the pauses. Only males that are already paired sing this song; yet you might have expected paired birds to reduce their singing, not sing feverishly at dawn. So what are they doing?

Studies of reed buntings reveal something else unusual about them. They are exceptionally prone to infidelity, far more so than most other small birds. While males and females form bonds similar to a marital arrangement in people, both sexes routinely indulge in copulations outside this pair bond. 'Routinely' might be an understatement: in fact 97 per cent of all females are known to indulge in extra-pair copulations; about 55 per cent of all DNA-assessed chicks in nests are from a different father to the social mate; and seeking sex in neighbouring territories accounted for 40 per cent of the average male's entire reproductive output. All these figures are much higher than for a bird such as a blue tit (fewer than 10 per cent of chicks sired outside the pair bond). It isn't clear why reed buntings are so

In 2009 a study in Sweden discovered something astonishing. They realized that, overlooked for a hundred years, the reed bunting doesn't just have two songs – it has three.

prone to this, although it might be related to their marshland habitat.

And what of those dawn songs? The obvious conclusion is that paired males singing at dawn are advertising their willingness to indulge in copulations outside the pair bond. Dawn is usually the time when a female is most fertile and receptive.

All the information is there to decode, if we care to listen to its songs.

Willow warbler

Phylloscopus trochilus

NORTHERN EURASIA; WINTERS IN SUB-SAHARAN AFRICA,
10.5–11.5 cm (AROUND 4 in)

 WE'RE WELL INTO MARCH AND THE BIRDS
in northern Eurasia are not being at all subtle
about the spring. The dawn chorus is swelling;
voices are rising. The secret is truly out, shouted
from the rooftops.

Amidst all the vehement verbiage, however, there is a quieter voice.
It is so gentle it is easily overlooked, but it seems to be sending a
message. 'Calm down. You call this spring? It's still pretty cold. Where
are all the leaves?'

The message comes from the willow warbler, and its authenticity
comes from the fact that it's a newcomer. This bird has wintered in
tropical Africa and now enters Europe and Asia, coloured by the
experience of warmer climes. In common with most small migrant
birds, males of its species compete to be first to the breeding areas;

the faster they get there, the better a territory they will acquire, with enhanced breeding prospects the prize. So, birds flood north at a pace that can be dangerous; if they arrive too early, they could easily succumb to starvation during March, the month that flatters to deceive.

The gorgeous song of the willow warbler, therefore, could be fancifully interpreted as one of caution. 'Don't write off the winter yet,' it implores as the other resident birds seem to be partying.

These days the willow warbler's song is usually the first transcontinental migrant to be heard in Northern Europe. Until recently, the chiffchaff (*Phylloscopus collybita*) and blackcap (*Sylvia atricapilla*) were treated as similar harbingers of spring, but climate change has meant that some individuals of these species overwinter in temperate zones and the species' pronouncements have lost their lustre. That has meant that the baton of vernal announcer has passed to the willow warbler.

The willow warbler's song is usually the first transcontinental migrant to be heard in northern Europe.

In truth, its song is completely perfect for the task. It is a gentle tiptoe up and down the scale, with an indeterminate ending that often blows away in the wind. The willow warbler's refusal to be loud and overconfident is deliciously apt, especially when sung, as it often is, from the earliest blossom of willow, its foliage respectfully subtle, redolent of the uncertain season.

However, the definitive gentleness of the willow warbler's song is a contradiction when it comes to the bird's overall behaviour. Competitive males are well known for their habit of fighting over territorial borders and some undoubtedly die during the mad rush for a place to breed. The song that whispers to us is a barrage of insults to the listeners that matter.

Male willow warblers usually have about two weeks to sort out their territorial borders before the females arrive, and most of this work is done by song. Once on site, the females listen carefully. It is thought that they pay particular attention to each male's rate of singing; it has been shown that the males that sing most frequently are the ones that pair up first, and the slouches must wait.

In recent years, scientific research has shown that the love lives of songbirds are much more complicated than we used to think, and the willow warbler is a good example of this. Some males don't just settle for one territory but have two instead. They attract a female early in the season and then once this primary mate is settled on the nest, incubating the clutch, these males move to a different place entirely and start singing there, hoping to attract another mate. As soon as this secondary mate is incubating, these 'scoundrels' abandon her and return to their first mate. They will then play good father and help feed the chicks.

The song of the willow warbler is gentle to our ears, but in the life of a songbird, the word is rarely a lived reality.

White-crowned sparrow

Zonotrichia leucophrys

NORTH AMERICA, 15–16 cm (AROUND 6 in)

IMAGINE YOU LOST YOUR BEARINGS WHILE exploring unfamiliar terrain in South Dakota, for example. If you were then to encounter a male white-crowned sparrow, you'd be able to position yourself instantly – if you were an expert in its song. Arguably, no bird in the world is as famous for its distinctive dialects. So with the right knowledge, you could narrow down your location to a matter of a few hundred metres, just by listening carefully. After a few song-phrases, you would know that you were close to Sioux Falls on the Iowan border, about 16 km (10 miles) out of town.

That songbirds have dialects has been known for many years. It is a product of how songs are learned. In some species, a song is simply inherited down the generations and doesn't vary much at all, in which case there are no dialects. In most songbirds, however, there is at least some learning. Usually, a bird has an internal template, which accounts for part of the song and ensures that it sounds like the correct species, while the rest is taken from external influences, such as the father or other local males. In the white-crowned sparrow, it is the local singers that matter. It copies them and, by trial and error, crystallizes its own song. Males of this species only have one song type, and it is typical of the location, and quite different from the song types of birds only a short distance away.

The sparrows, not surprisingly, easily distinguish other song types, so that they are instantly aware of intruders. They can tell whether a rival is a neighbour or a stranger, and whether it is their own subspecies of white-crowned sparrow or a different species of sparrow altogether. The females, for their part, have varying sexual responses to diverse songs.

These female responses are important. It has been shown that females aren't just attracted by male song. It also stimulates them to start nest building and has the internal effect of growing the ovaries prior to breeding. Presumably this doesn't happen when a female hears a stranger's song.

One of the corollaries to such strong recognition is that, in some populations, gene flow could be restricted because of the refusal

The sparrows easily distinguish other song types, so that they are instantly aware of intruders. They can tell whether a rival is a neighbour or a stranger, and whether it is their own subspecies of white-crowned sparrow or a different species of sparrow altogether.

of birds to interbreed with those of other dialects, and the general aggression towards strangers.

Some males are bilingual. Normally hatched on the border between two dialect zones, these males sing two different songs, each from the two zones. This presumably increases their chances of finding at least one mate.

Quite what might happen if a bird hatches on the boundary between three territories isn't known!

Common nightingale

Luscinia megarhynchos

CENTRAL EUROPE AND NORTH AFRICA EAST TO MONGOLIA;
MIGRATES TO SUB-SAHARAN AFRICA IN WINTER,
16–17 cm (AROUND 6½ in)

THERE IS PERHAPS NO MORE FAMOUS songster in the Western world than the nightingale. Even in the Americas, where there are a few world-class singers (see wood thrush, page 68, and northern mockingbird, page 120), some species, such as the nightingale wren (*Microcerculus philomela*), are named in its honour. Its fame has spread far beyond its range, such that you don't need to have heard its song to be familiar with its name. The nightingale represents the best in birdsong, its zenith, perhaps its fulfilment. A veritable avalanche of culture insists that hearing a nightingale transcends the act of listening to a bird and brings you to a special place.

That avalanche of culture can be a problem when you take people on a special expedition to hear the bird. Part of my own job, as a professional guide, is to do just that. I always go with hesitation, and I carefully monitor the reaction of the people who come along. Eventually the bird sings and there is always delight, and often wonder. But sometimes it feels like a letdown. The reality is that the nightingale sings with an exceptional dynamic range and variety, with up to 600 different elements, and it is glorious to listen to. There are sections that are unique: the wonderful introductory, accelerating crescendo that is often described as 'sobbing'; the passages that must surely end with an exclamation mark; the sudden switch from tender to triumphant. It is a fantastic performance and a real experience.

But is it really worth its pedestal, I wonder? There are numerous fine avian singers. Many species might not be as spectacular and technically brilliant as the nightingale, but they lift my own heart more. There must be many out there who like the mastersinger, but don't truly love it.

The English poet John Keats obviously wasn't one of these. Hearing the bird lifted him to barely surpassed romantic literary heights. Here is an extract from his celebrated poem 'Ode to a Nightingale', written in Hampstead, London, in 1819.

'Tis not through envy of thy happy lot,
But being too happy in thine happiness, –
That thou, light-winged Dryad of the trees
In some melodious plot
Of beechen green, and shadows numberless,
Singest of summer in full-throated ease.

The trouble is that laying this finest of culture upon a mere singing bird lifts our expectations so sky high that they are impossible to meet. The problem with hearing the bird for the first time in the wild is that, in your mind, you have heard it before.

Having said that, there are several other reasons why a nightingale is special. The first is that it sings at night, as the name implies, although it sings just as much during the day, unbeknownst to many. This nocturnal singing is quite unusual, although far from unique, for a songbird. What tends to happen is that you arrive in nightingale habitat in the evening, and the rest of the bird chorus dwindles, as if they are the warm-up act for the main event. Only in the comparative silence does the nightingale sing, uninterrupted by 'inferiors'.

A second feature of nightingale song is that it is best at the most romantic time of the year, in heavy spring. It's heard against a backdrop of blossom-covered thickets and fresh green leaves, sometimes with a carpet of wildflowers; a backdrop of universal hope, delight and excitement. The song stirs you, but it actually stirs an already heady brew of emotions.

And finally, the nightingale holds a secret: it makes its song rare. By that I don't mean that it doesn't give its all when it arrives on territory or reduces its song rate compared with other birds. I mean that its season is short. It arrives in April and is usually silent by June, and after those months it more or less disappears when breeding and retreats quietly to Africa in August. Its singing is at a premium, and that's part of the reason why it's special. We might think, *if it is so brief, did it really happen?*

As John Keats himself says:

Adieu! adieu! thy plaintive anthem fades
Past the near meadows, over the still stream,
Up the hill-side; and now 'tis buried deep
In the next valley-glades:
Was it a vision, or a waking dream?
Fled is that music: – Do I wake or sleep?

Sedge warbler

Acrocephalus schoenobaenus

EUROPE AND WESTERN ASIA; MIGRATES TO SUB-SAHARAN
AFRICA IN WINTER, 13 cm (5 in)

IF EVER A BIRD AND ITS SONG WERE
symptomatic of the hurry of spring, it would be
the turbo-charged sedge warbler, at this moment
singing manically from marshes and weedy areas
all over Europe. The advance of the warmer season
in the northern hemisphere is currently exponential, having been slow
and careful in March. Now everything explodes. Whereas a couple of
weeks ago we were enjoying the first signs of spring, now we've been
plunged headlong into it, with its universal business. It is everywhere;
the signposts have been washed away in a surge of noise and activity.

The sedge warbler fizzes with this energy. It is a life force of spring
and, as we shall see, a suitably brief one, too. Its very being seems to
be saying, 'Hurry up, hurry up!' The song, sung only by the male, is
a whirl of scratchy and sweet phrases jumbled together into a rapid

monologue a minute or so long, including a fair amount of mimicry. At the start, you get the impression that the bird just wants to speed up, like a vehicle fitted only with an accelerator.

The bird's actions during singing only magnify the notion of haste. A sedge warbler often starts a song bout out of sight, hidden in a thorny bush on the edge of a reedbed, for example, or a bog or patch of scrub. As it gets going, however, it gradually makes its way upwards, towards the top of the

The song, sung only by the male, is a whirl of scratchy and sweet phrases jumbled together into a rapid monologue.

bush, forever inching higher until, at last, it reaches the top and shows itself. The bird sings with all its being, the performance enhanced by the fact that the inside of its mouth is red.

Typically, the bush is not enough to contain it. After several impatient minutes the sedge warbler finally does what its twitchiness has promised and launches into the air, still singing. Aloft, it beats its wings wildly, yet the display is invariably a letdown, at least to the human observer. The singer doesn't fly high, nor does it fly for long. It just seems to flip up and dive down into the reedbeds. But within a few moments, its dignity restored, the sedge warbler is back shouting unseen from the lower branches, before spiralling upwards perch by perch, its performance a helter-skelter of furious energy. If birds were ever to sweat (which they don't), the sedge warbler would be the one to show it.

As ever with spring songs, there is an audience listening and watching, and its reaction matters. Female sedge warblers are choosy, but they too are in a hurry. It doesn't take long to monitor a male by song – that, after all, is what a song is for – and there is plenty of information contained in each male's proclamations to guide them. They don't even need to meet the male face to face. Like many species, the repertoire matters. Those lively, scratchy notes, the flourishes of mimicry, that 'sweep' note here and that rattling there – all combine to describe the singer's versatility. Male sedge warblers with rich repertoires pair up first; invention is inviting.

Even the pathetic song flight matters. Scientists have discovered that there is a link between the sheer number of song flights that a male sedge warbler performs while it is singing and its state of health. The less lively birds were found to have more blood parasites, a reliable indicator of their overall fitness.

On the whole, a female songbird has a limited range of males to choose from – somewhere between five and ten – so the song is a key indicator of a suitable mate.

Sedge warblers pair up quickly, and then something unusual happens: the males stop singing altogether. The song has performed its key function and the marshy margins fall silent. In the case of most other species, males keep singing when they have paired in order to defend both territory and paternity. But the sedge warbler has shut the door on its singing effort.

Many sedge warblers have fallen silent by May. The loss of this effervescent performer from the airwaves is something of a turning point. It is perhaps the first sign that spring is not eternal, not this year. All the other birds eventually follow suit, and the wondrous madness comes to an end.

That isn't to say that the silence signals any kind of pause for the sedge warbler. It speeds eggs into nests, feeds its young as if they were mass-produced and, fair winds permitting, might squeeze two broods into a season (although it is usually only one). The feverish bird is never still. And neither is the passage of spring.

Wood thrush

Hylocichla mustelina

EASTERN NORTH AMERICA; MIGRATES TO CENTRAL
AMERICA, 19–20 cm (7½–8 in)

THIS ESSAY SHOULD PROBABLY BE ABOUT
the hermit thrush (*Catharus guttatus*). Arguably, it
has a better song than the wood thrush – sometimes
referred to as 'the American nightingale' – and it is
certainly found over a greater part of the continent
than its eastern relative. But the appreciation of birdsong is intensely
personal, and the wood thrush tips it for me. Why don't you listen
to both and make up your own mind? They are, after all, two of the
most utterly gorgeous bird songs in the world. Both are currently
singing from the woods and forests, 'pouring silver chords from the
impenetrable shadows', in the words of Aldo Leopold, the great
American writer and environmentalist.

As it happens, I'm gratefully in the same camp as the celebrated
American poet and writer Henry Thoreau. He would regularly hear the

wood thrush in his cabin near Concord, Massachusetts, and left some memorable observations in his *Journal*, which he kept from 1837 to 1861. Here, for starters, is a testament to the power of birdsong to the emotions, written in July 1852:

'The wood thrush's is no opera music; it is not so much the composition as the strain, the tone – cool bars of melody from the atmosphere of everlasting morning or evening ... The thrush alone declares the immortal wealth and vigor that is in the forest ... Whenever a man hears it, he is young, and Nature is in her spring. Wherever he hears it, it is a new world and a free country, and the gates of heaven are not shut against him.'

All of us can testify to the way in which bird songs can free us the from the worries of this world and the constraints of our life, and even contribute to our well-being, but few of us can make such poetry of it.

In June 1853, Thoreau wrote about an enchanting encounter with the wood thrush: 'This is the only bird whose notes affect me like music. It lifts and exhilarates me. It is inspiring. It changes all hours to an eternal morning.'

Unbeknownst to Thoreau, he was unerringly correct in his musical assessment of the wood thrush. The song does indeed follow a natural human scale.

In another part of his journal, he attempts to describe the song in more detail, saying: 'He launches forth one strain with all his heart and life and soul, of pure and unmatchable melody, and then he pauses and gives the hearer and himself time to digest this, and then another and another at suitable intervals.'

Anybody who has heard the wood thrush singing will instantly identify with Thoreau's description of the unhurried nature of the song, where every phrase is sung perfectly and there's time to revel in its beauty before it moves on to the next.

You might expect that scientific analysis would break down this natural wonder into constituent ordinariness and sully its beauty. But happily it doesn't do this. Instead, it reveals a simplicity and technical order that only makes you marvel more.

There are three parts to each wood thrush phrase, A, B and C: A is the introductory, short, low-pitched series of 'bup' notes; B is the glorious, skirling, ethereal middle; and C is the terminal trill. All three sections may vary: an average wood thrush will have 1–3 A sections, 2–8 B sections and 6–12 C sections in its repertoire. Then it simply mixes them up, and the result is pure magic.

Interestingly, the loudest section, the middle (B), is copied from all the other wood thrushes in the area, so is local and recognized by other males in the vicinity. The A and C sections are thought to be either innate or are invented by the individual. Few bird songs are so easy to appreciate and understand.

Scientific analysis has revealed something else about the wood thrush song that is even more thrilling and remarkable. If you slow down the song on a recording system and produce a diagram of pitch against time (a sonogram), something extraordinary is revealed. The wood thrush is able to produce two separate elements to its song at the same time – they overlap!

In contrast to the voice of a human, which comes from the vocal chords in the windpipe, or trachea, bird songs arise from an organ called a syrinx, which is situated at the bottom of the trachea, where the two bronchi branch into the respective left and right lungs. Owing to its position at the junction of two air passages, the syrinx can utilize two airflows at the same time. What we hear from some birds, therefore, is the composite of two songs at once. The wood thrush duets with itself. No wonder it produces such a masterpiece.

Common cuckoo

Cuculus canorus

WIDESPREAD SUMMER VISITOR TO EURASIA; WINTERS
IN SUB-SAHARAN AFRICA AND INDIA, 32–34 cm (12½–13¼ in)

 IT'S AMAZING WHAT A COUPLE OF SONOROUS
notes will do. Every spring, the common cuckoo
arrives as a migrant all over Europe and northern
Asia, and gives off its loud 'Cuck-oo' advertising call.
Evocative and far-carrying, this simple sound has
spawned a veritable deluge of colourful human culture and tradition.

The voice echoing through the woods, fields and open country has
an irresistible connection with the change in season, with the arrival of
spring. In the Czech Republic, they say: 'The swallow brings the spring,
but the cuckoo brings warm days.' And it's true. The swallow often
arrives during the chill wind; but the cuckoo, usually arriving in mid-
April at least, is not the harbinger of spring, but its consummation.

Across many cultures, the hearing of the first cuckoo is a significant
personal event, and over the course of centuries it has been associated

with good or bad luck. In Germany, you had better take out your wallet and shake it when you first hear the cuckoo, so that your financial fortunes will smile; if you don't, they will nosedive. In France, you also need money in your pocket at the seminal moment, and in Bulgaria, you need a full stomach and available money. These matters will seal your fortunes for the year.

In Ukraine, the cuckoo's arrival predicts the harvest. If the bird calls when the leaves are already green, that's a good sign that all will be well; but if the leaves are bare, it predicts nothing short of calamity and disaster – so, no half-measures there. In Armenia, just in case you haven't been paying attention, the cuckoos might start calling more intensively towards late spring, and this is a warning that the harvest time is drawing near, so listen out.

The folk tales aren't only concerned with money and prosperity; your first meeting with a cuckoo this year might be a matter of life and death. In Greece, a first 'cuckooing' when you happen to have a full stomach ensures that you won't be needing a doctor for the next year, but if you're hungry at the time, you might need to look out for your symptoms. Or, more alarmingly, in several countries you need to pay attention to your first cuckoo, because the number of calls it gives counts out the remaining years of your life.

Cuckoos, not surprisingly given the times at which they call, are also believed to predict your romantic success. In Ukraine, a cuckoo calling outside your house predicts a wedding, so long as it's perched on a guelder rose shrub. But when you hear a cuckoo in Bulgaria, I'm afraid the time has come to stop flirting with whoever you have your eye on and get into the fields to work!

The Swedes cover their bases in what might be described as a fatalistic Scandi-noir fashion. The first cuckoo in the north brings grief, in the south brings death, in the east brings solace and in the west it's best.

Not surprisingly, the cult of the cuckoo has leaked into many art forms, including inventions. In the Black Forest in southern Germany, from about 1740 they began a cottage industry making clocks that struck the hours with a mechanical mechanism that pinged out a toy bird to render the hour. Apparently, the initial intention was to use the call of a cockerel (see page 84), that universal clarion call of time moving on, but the cuckoo has a simpler song, so it took its place and has been there ever since.

Cuckoos have found their way into numerous pieces of music, art and literature. One of the most famous is undoubtedly a brief but starring role in Ludwig van Beethoven's Symphony No. 6, 'Pastoral', which was premiered in 1808. At the end of the second movement, the Scene by the Brook, two clarinets represent the call of the cuckoo, superimposed on a quail (oboe) and nightingale (flute). It is gorgeously redolent of the countryside around Vienna, where the composer, a great lover of the countryside and wildlife, would frequently walk. While the species are symbolic of love (nightingale), God's provision (quail) and the coming of spring (cuckoo), there is little doubt that Beethoven was deeply familiar with all three species. Indeed, it is fun to speculate on whether he ever heard all these birds vocalizing at once – it is definitely possible. If he did, there was only a narrow window of time and season when it could be done. The quail doesn't sing much during the day, so it is almost certainly a late evening encounter; and it almost certainly happened in May, when all three species are most likely to be at their vocal peak – probably in the first week.

On the occasion the symphony was first performed, the cuckoo didn't bring Beethoven much luck. Chronically under-rehearsed, the event was a disaster. Indeed, the composer probably heard his first cuckoo on an empty stomach in 1808, and without coins in his pocket.

Marsh wren

Cistothorus palustris

NORTH AMERICA, 10–14 cm (4–5½ in)

ENOUGH OF THIS LOVELINESS; IT'S TIME TO celebrate a bird song that, to our ears, really isn't very good at all. The ornithological founding fathers of the USA weren't very complimentary about the song of the marsh wren. Alexander Wilson described it as 'deficient and contemptible', while John James Audubon snidely and sarcastically said: 'the song – *if song I may call it ...*' (italics and sympathy mine). Oh dear. Does anyone hear this bird on a good day?

If you've heard the marsh wren's song, you are more likely to be amused than disgusted. It's a rollicking delight. At this time of year, go to a marsh crowned with flowering bulrushes almost anywhere in North America, and you'll be in for a treat. You'll hear rattles, gurgles, bubbles, little whirrs, splutters and mechanical flatulent sounds. Some of the songs have been aptly compared to the rhythmic whirring of an old-fashioned sewing machine, the zinger doing a Singer. Close your eyes and you could liken the wetland around you to a graveyard for clockwork toys breathing their last. Marsh wren immersion is cathartic, I promise you.

The ornithologists of long ago who dismissed the marsh wren overlooked something that truly defines the bird itself: it is a trier. It is effort encapsulated in a living being. In the midst of the season, about now, marsh wrens typically sing all night long, as if they were excited children on a sleepover. At times, there can barely be any gaps between these volleys of volubility (like excited children ...). The sheer commitment to singing is, from a distance, quite exhausting.

It is effort encapsulated in a living being. In the midst of the season, marsh wrens typically sing all night long.

Marsh wren behaviour shows up something that we might not really appreciate about the reality of the breeding season for a wild animal. It can be a bit desperate. Our forebears, and some contemporary writers, liked to think that birdsong is an expression of happiness. But the biology doesn't stack up. It is impossible to gauge whether a bird is enjoying itself, because you cannot measure it. A bird might feel bullish when singing if it is having success with females, but that doesn't equate to happiness.

Furthermore, the very function of song is competitive. Males sing to establish a territory and attract a mate. A bird with a territory excludes other males without a place to call their own. Some males, even with territories, go without a mate. You only need to listen to the marsh wrens at full tilt to appreciate their fervour. One male sings and another is stimulated to sing immediately, often before the phrase of the other has finished, the two struggling for their voice to prevail. This tit for tat is known as counter-singing. In particularly aggressive encounters, one bird sings a certain song type and the other sings exactly the same, which is known as 'matched counter-singing'. It means 'I sing this phrase better than you do'.

The mêlée of the marsh wrens is especially ferocious because females are interested in quality, not exclusivity. Some male marsh wrens pair up with two females and some three. But that means that some birds don't pair up at all and are doomed to a season of failure. In a study in Manitoba, there were ten bachelors, 53 monogamists, 48 bigamists and nine trigamists. In a perfect world in which song was happy, the nine trigamists would have allowed their females to pair up with the bachelors!

But that's not how it works. It's a competition, and at times it's probably desperate. The birds are seized by energy because the cost of failure is so high. They may not live to next season. It could be their only chance to breed.

So go out into a marsh this season and enjoy this vocal mayhem. Just don't expect the birds to do the same.

Eastern whip-poor-will

Antrostomus vociferus

NORTH AMERICA; MIGRATES TO WINTER AS FAR SOUTH
AS COSTA RICA, 22–25 cm (8½–10 in)

EUROPEAN FILM-MAKERS HAVE OWLS;
Americans have whip-poor-wills. The owls are
melancholic, the whip-poor-will is strange and
unsettling, but both are ideal if you wish to convey
an atmosphere of nocturnal menace.

The eastern whip-poor-will should be an obscure bird, whose
existence barely registers on the human radar. It is medium-sized and
brown with intense barring; and it hides away during the day using
cryptic camouflage that's so effective you would struggle to see it on
your lawn, let alone on the woodland floor, where it resides during
the daylight hours. Keen birdwatchers are lucky if they manage to see
one on a dedicated nocturnal whip-poor-will hunt with torches and
car headlights, so the chances of the general public stumbling upon it
are negligible.

Yet this spectre has found its way into the American psyche by way of its loud, clear and repetitive advertising call. It really does sound exactly like its common name, the perfect onomatopoeia. There is a slight pause between the 'whip' and the 'poor-will', and

This spectre has found its way into the American psyche by way of its loud, clear and repetitive advertising call.

hardly a breath between one phrase and the other. The overall song is a clear, liquid whistle.

It is the bird's former abundance, now much reduced, that really put this member of the nightjar family (see page 104) into people's consciousness, and it is particularly resonant of the rural south. It has found its way into literature, such as Harper Lee's *To Kill a Mockingbird* and Washington Irving's *The Legend of Sleepy Hollow*. It is featured in music, too, such as Hank Williams's ballad 'I'm So Lonesome I Could Cry,' in which the songwriter evidently came upon a particularly downtrodden individual: 'Hear that lonesome whippoorwill, he sounds too blue to fly.' More romantically, in Frank Capra's 1934 romcom *It Happened One Night*, Clark Gable declares to Claudette Colbert: 'I am the whip-poor-will that cries in the night.' And the bird song itself, recorded in the wild, has found its way into multiple movie moments of Deep South terror, making a welcome change from the shivering call of the common loon (*Gavia immer*), which actually breeds on lakes in the north of the continent.

There is another cultural reference that provides an enlightening take on this disembodied voice. In *The Whip-Poor-Will*, a short story by American author and humorist James Thurber, the protagonist is kept awake at night by the incessant calling of the whip-poor-will, and this eventually drives him mad – so much so that he goes on a killing spree.

The macabre tale does draw attention to the whip-poor-will's tendency to repeat its name to an extraordinary extent. There is one report of a bird calling 1,088 times at a rapid pace without a break. I suppose if you weren't delighted to hear one, this could drive you insane.

A few years ago, on 7 May 2001, the legendary bird-song expert and writer Don Kroodsma set out one night to see just how often this bird did repeat its famous phrase. He stayed up throughout the hours of darkness near his home in Massachusetts, following a singing bird on foot and by bike, and literally counted how often this single bird called. He says: 'I add up my hourly tallies: 2,500 (from 8:10 to 9:00 p.m.), 1,680, 2,570, 2,112, 2,344, 2,007, 2,440, 2,466, 2,590, + 189 for the few minutes after 5:00 a.m. equals 20,898 songs. Two-zero-eight-nine-eight. Twenty thousand, eight hundred ninety-eight.'

The very repeating of the figure conveys the sheer wonder Kroodsma feels at the indefatigability of his subject. Perhaps it also shows how, in this world, you can get noticed.

Red junglefowl

Gallus gallus

INDIA AND SOUTHEAST ASIA EAST TO THE PHILIPPINES;
DOMESTICATED WORLDWIDE, 41–78 cm (16–31 in)

MUCH IS MADE OF THE SWEETNESS OF THE dawn chorus. But, in truth, there is one species of bird on the planet that proclaims daybreak to more human ears than any other – and that is the humble cockerel, the male of a bird we universally know as the chicken. Its ancestor is a bird that is still at large widely over India and Southeast Asia, where it goes by the name of the red junglefowl.

The crowing of the red junglefowl and the cockerel aren't quite the same. The junglefowl's call sounds much more sore-throated, and the triumphant emphasis that is so familiar at the end of a cockerel's advertising is not quite there. However, even without seeing the very smart wild bird, you can immediately detect the similarity; and the crowing in the wild, as in dusty settlements around the world, is also mostly uttered at dawn and dusk.

It is thought that people domesticated junglefowl at least 5,000 years ago, and over the years it is highly likely that more people have heard this bird call than any other in human history. Currently the species is ubiquitous and generally considered to be the most numerous bird in the world, with an estimated population (most of it captive) of 23 billion – well in excess of the human population. It plays a vital, if unhappy, role in feeding our world.

But in its role as a living alarm clock, the cockerel has become deeply symbolic to humankind. As American writer Henry Thoreau wrote in the July 1852 entry of his *Journal*: 'As I came along, the whole earth resounded with the crowing of cocks, from the eastern until the western horizon, and as I passed a yard, I saw a white rooster on the topmost rail of a fence pouring forth his challenges for destiny to come on. This salutation was travelling round the world.'

It is thought that people domesticated junglefowl at least 5,000 years ago, and it is likely that more people have heard this bird call than any other in human history.

The crowing of the cock summons the dawn and provides us with renewed freshness, a chance of a new start every day. It is nature's reset. Until the day is lived, we cannot know how it will go, so the crowing of the cock tends to be a symbol of optimism and possibility – and indeed challenge. It also gives a chance at redemption. In the unforgettable account of Christ's Passion in the gospels of the New Testament, Jesus predicts that his disciple Peter will deny being a follower of his three times on that terrible night 'before the cock crows'. And so it turns out; in his fear for his own life, it is only when he hears the crowing that Peter realizes what he has done. Yet the voice of the dawn also brings an end to the chapter of Peter's denial and sets him up for his reinstatement as a disciple later in the text.

Not only does the cockerel summon the dawn and give us, once again, a chance at life; it also banishes the night, and all that that implies. As the great English playwright William Shakespeare reminds us in *Hamlet*, as we welcome dawn, we can also be relieved that the nocturnal terrors are fleeing:

> *The cock, that is the trumpet to the morn,*
> *Doth with his lofty and shrill-sounding throat*
> *Awake the god of day; and at his warning,*
> *Whether in sea or fire, in earth or air,*
> *Th'extravagant and erring spirit hies*
> *To his confine; ...*

And, let's face it, we can all be relieved that the erring spirits are, for a time at least, cowering in the light of day.

In the light of this, you may think that everybody would appreciate the familiar sound, but there is a truth somewhat missing from passionate literature: some people notably dislike their slumber being disturbed. Apparently, the human world is made up of larks who wake up naturally and owls who function well at night. Every day, billions quietly curse the zealous cockerel.

This dislike reached the headlines in the UK a few years ago, when a lawyer who had moved into a sleepy countryside village discovered that it wasn't as sleepy as he thought and tried to sue his neighbours for the misdemeanour of owning a cockerel that invaded his sensibilities. He probably spoke for many, but felicitously he lost his case.

Chestnut-sided warbler

Setophaga pensylvanica

EASTERN NORTH AMERICA; MIGRATES TO WINTER AROUND THE
CARIBBEAN AS FAR SOUTH AS NORTH-WEST SOUTH AMERICA,
10–14 cm (4–5½ in)

THERE IS A STORY TO TELL WITHIN THE short but enthusiastic phrases of the chestnut-sided warbler. A great favourite among American birders, owing largely to its unusual and very attractive plumage, this diminutive and lively sprite nonetheless utters a cheery and upbeat song, which everybody remembers as 'Pleased, pleased, pleased to MEETCHA'. The flourish at the end is usually the clincher.

Except, it isn't always – sometimes the bird doesn't 'meetcha' at all. Sometimes it's just 'pleased'. Listening uncritically to the bird in the wild, you might think that sometimes the male chestnut-sided warbler just forgets to put its usual upbeat flourish on the end – after all, there is a territory to defend and feeding to do. It could be distracted.

But no, that's not the case. The chestnut-sided warbler has two different song types, labelled by scientists as having an accented ending (AE – the familiar 'meetcha' song) and an unaccented ending (UE – the reduced song.) This, as Charles Dickens didn't say, is a tale of two ditties.

Although the distinction sounds subtle to our ears, scientists have found that the two songs have quite different functions and divergent origins, and that they are intended for two separate audiences. One song is aimed at male listeners, namely rivals, and one song is delivered hopefully to female listeners – to the mate or potential mate.

When a male arrives on the breeding grounds in spring, it launches into almost continuous song. It might even sing 250 times an hour, about four times a minute. Interestingly, at this stage it only sings AE songs, the familiar one, or adds the odd UE song every so often. Among many transcontinental spring migrants of the northern hemisphere, it is typical for the males to arrive well before the females, often a couple of weeks ahead, and the chestnut-sided warbler is no exception. So, since the arrivals all begin by singing AE songs, it is reasonable to assume that they are intended for rival males. As time moves on, the males set up territories while they await the arrival of females.

Once the females arrive, UE songs begin to echo across the scrubby habitats where these birds breed. Once they pair up, the males sing more of this type. On a given day in the breeding season, male chestnut-sided warblers arise at dawn and join in the chorus. For about half an hour, they almost entirely utter their UE songs, before switching to majority AE songs for the rest of the day. We can conclude that, whatever chestnut-sided warblers are saying during the dawn chorus, it is directed at mates and not rivals. The singers' most pressing concern, their most urgent sunrise message, is to their mates. Female birds tend to be at their most fertile at dawn, so the males are wise to keep talking, assuring their mates that they are very much around and in possession.

Careful analysis of the two songs has revealed some startling results. In the laboratory, scientists found that a hand-reared male would sing its AE song innately. On the other hand, hand-reared males would not acquire UE songs unless they were provided with a live tutor. The scientists also found that males with tutors would begin to improvise their own songs.

As you might have picked up from other parts of this book, it pays a singing bird to improvise. A good repertoire is usually an honest reflection of good quality. Having a good repertoire of UE songs should appeal to females.

But why use the inherited AE song at all, when all the excitement is in the UE song? Well, a bird's first task upon arriving on territory is to send a simple message to other males that it has arrived. There needn't be much invention – it's all a matter of intention. The song rate and vehemence could be a good guide to an individual's fitness and strength of purpose.

When the females arrive, however, a chestnut-sided warbler needs to do more. It needs to be creative to stand out from the crowd.

But the AE song is also an insurance policy. While most males return to the place of their birth in spring, females are far more likely to wander in the early breeding season. If males sing a standardized song, not subject to individual and local variation, they will at least put down a marker for newly arrived females that male members of their species are around.

And fascinatingly, when scientists listened to chestnut-sided warbler recordings from times past, they found that AE songs have barely changed in years, while UE songs change with time and fashion.

The more things change, the more they remain the same.

Common hawk-cuckoo

Hierococcyx varius

INDIA EAST TO THAILAND AND SRI LANKA,
35 cm (ABOUT 13 in)

PEOPLE EVERYWHERE CAN TESTIFY TO the wonderfully nourishing effect of bird songs. Throughout time, people have revelled in the natural choruses around the world. The sounds of birds have inspired peasants, poets, people with gilded lives and people in terrible want. In recent times, it has even been proven that the sound of birdsong helps people with mental health issues (see page 34) or comforts those who are simply struggling with life.

Well, tell all that to the people of India, or indeed other parts of southern Asia. They will counter with the observation that birdsong is not always a good thing – sometimes it's a nuisance. And as for mental health, they say, it's true that sometimes it makes you feel better. But there is one bird, unfortunately, that makes you feel much worse.

May I introduce you to the common hawk-cuckoo? Or, since many people only know it by its nickname, would you care to meet the 'brain-fever bird'?

'I just hate it,' says a friend. 'This brain-fever bird never stops calling, sometimes day and night. Before the monsoon, the sound of it seems to embody the overall tension in the air.'

To understand why this bird sound evokes such a reaction, you really need to listen to it. Immediately, you will be struck by its loudness and its repetitive nature, calling in series of ten or more. Many have described it as a shriek, which is unkind, since it is more of a loud whistle. What truly sets it apart is that as the song progresses it both speeds up and becomes higher pitched. This gives a real impression of rising panic. 'Come on,' it says at the start. Then it becomes less polite: 'Come ON!' Finally, its entreaties become shriller and more insistent, as if the bird were about to blow its top. You begin to fear for its sanity, knowing that its needs will never become less urgent.

As the song progresses it both speeds up and becomes higher pitched. This gives a real impression of rising panic.

Now, imagine having to listen to that call all day – or worse, as is common, through a moonlit night. Imagine that night is muggy, and the meteorological atmosphere is heavy. In such circumstances, it is easy to identify with the person who does not find this natural sound helpful for their state of mind!

It would be tempting to say that, away from its job of driving people insane, the common hawk-cuckoo lives a blameless life. But, of course, that all depends on how you might interpret its lifestyle. It is anthropomorphic to attach some kind of malevolence to a bird that merely follows its evolutionary imperatives, but it is nonetheless a member of the cuckoo family and is parasitic. It lays its eggs in the nests of other birds, subcontracting the care of its own to unknowing hosts – mainly members of a widespread, primarily Asian family known as the babblers (see page 174). The young make begging calls closely resembling the young of the hosts.

It lays its eggs in the nests of other birds, subcontracting the care of its own to unknowing hosts.

And when they grow up, humans will be begging them to stop.

Brown thrasher

Toxostoma rufum

EASTERN NORTH AMERICA, 23–30 cm (9–12 in)

IT CAN BE A PROBLEM TO HAVE A MORE famous relative. America should be celebrating the brown thrasher, one of the most inventive vocalists in the world of birds. But instead, everybody has heard of the mockingbird (see page 120) and almost nobody, keen birdwatchers aside, has much to do with its cousin. There is no book *To Kill a Thrasher*; the mocker has put the mockers on the thrasher's bid at fame.

In truth, the brown thrasher has always been too retiring to be a truly iconic species. Even when singing, it often remains out of sight. The mockingbird struts across your lawn, while the thrasher prefers to skulk in the vegetation. The mockingbird has a look-at-me attitude, while that of the thrasher is 'look away' and it concentrates on its incredible vocal abilities, talented but diffident.

That said, the brown thrasher is a common bird of eastern North American, and its song is familiar enough. It is a long phrase that could be described as rambling, but that doesn't do justice to its clear diction and endless variety. Each element of song is repeated, on average, 1.5 times within a soliloquy with no structured beginning or ending, but with definite gaps between elements. It just starts, speaks and carries on until it randomly stops.

It's easy to assign words or phrases to a thrasher's song. You can invent your own. How about: 'Hear me, hear me, brown thrasher, brown thrasher, I'm lost, I'm lost, can you find me? Thick scrub, thick scrub, low down, low down ...'. But yours will be just as good as mine.

You can invent your own, because the male brown thrasher invents its own song. It literally makes it up as it goes along, something that is vanishingly rare among songbirds. Some elements are reused, but not until a long break from their previous airing. At least some motifs are copied from other birds, but it seems that there are very few of these. There doesn't seem to be much copying or learning from other thrashers either.

The brown thrasher has the widest repertoire of any bird species known in the world. Researchers have found that a male may use 2,000 different motifs, and quite possibly 3,000.

The result of this is remarkable. The brown thrasher has the widest repertoire of any bird species known in the world. Researchers have found that a male may use 2,000 different motifs, and quite possibly 3,000, many of which would appear to be unique to the individual. Not surprisingly, female thrashers respond favourably to males with large repertoires.

These factors make it all the more unfair that, in human eyes, the brown thrasher lies in the shadow of the mockingbird. The bird itself is arguably much more attractive than its relative, too, with rich, bold, chestnut colouration and heavy black streaks on the breast. And purists would point to its song

Each element of song is repeated, on average, 1.5 times within a soliloquy with no structured beginning or ending.

being slower, fruitier and richer than the mockingbird's. Being gifted, if seems, only gets you so far; chutzpah gets you further.

Yellowhammer

Emberiza citrinella

EURASIA EAST TO MONGOLIA, 16–16.5 cm (ABOUT 6½ in)

AS WE REACH THE SUMMER SOLSTICE, those of us in the northern hemisphere tilt towards shorter days. The spring is very much over, and the season of birdsong is also winding down. The jumble of sounds typified by the dawn chorus has already almost ceased, with just a few species that try multiple breeding attempts making desultory efforts at song.

In such times, it is deeply refreshing to know that a few birds are seemingly deaf to the silence and, despite the season, are still singing lustily. In Europe, one of these blessed birds is the yellowhammer. It is multiple-brooded and the male, almost alone among the hedgerow birds, is seized with the need to keep going. In fact, on a June day it might repeat its dry ditty 7,000 times.

Its tendency to sing all summer long has been noted by writers and poets. In his poem 'The Leprechaun or Fairy Shoemaker' the Irish poet William Allingham writes thus:

Little Cowboy, what have you heard
Up on the lonely rath's green mound?
Only the plaintive yellow bird
Sighing in sultry fields around,
Chary, chary, chary, chee-ee! –
Only the grasshopper and the bee? –

The yellowhammer does indeed sing when the only accompaniment is the chirping of grasshoppers and the buzzing of bees. Allingham's fictional description of the song – 'Chary, chary, chary, chee' – isn't bad, although most British readers are likely to be used to this longer interpretation: 'A little bit of bread and no cheese'. Another description is of a bird singing a phrase of dry notes and then running out of breath, inhaling heavily at the end.

Despite the yellowhammer's delightful commitment to singing into the sultry summer and during the afternoon, it doesn't escape from the usual scrutiny that plagues every songbird. The madness of early season might be over, but the overall competitiveness is far from done. A male still needs to sound good and look good if it is to keep the attention of its mate.

Singing a song is deeply exposing for a bird, because it can only do as well as its physical makeup allows. Singing is a little bit like publishing your work, with the birds around you – both rival males and potential female mates – acting as your reviewers. They are brutal; the one thing a wild bird cannot do, with its short life and compulsion to pass on its genetic material, is give the benefit of the doubt, so your male rivals will oust you and your potential mates will ignore you. In yellowhammer life, your song must come up to scratch. If your repertoire is deficient in comparison with your peers, or if you simply don't sing with necessary vigour, your breeding potential – your very raison d'être – is compromised.

As a yellowhammer, your song must pass muster and you must also pass the mustard test. You have to ensure that you are yellow enough, literally – and, indeed, have some red in your plumage as well. Female yellowhammers notice red. The 'yellow breast and head of solid gold' in Romantic poet John Clare's 'The Yellowhammer' isn't enough.

A bird's body chemistry cannot make yellow pigments in the course of routine physiology. Instead, they must come from the environment, which of course takes effort. The main source of the required carotenoids is plant leaves, but since yellowhammers don't eat leaves directly, they must consume leaf-eaters instead – mainly caterpillars. It is probably something of a pain to spend your moulting period (usually July) looking for caterpillars, when there are abundant other sources of food available in the summer, but there you are – it will pay off next spring. Experiments have shown that the more carotenoids a bird consumes, the yellower it becomes.

Red pigments, which may crop up in various parts of the bird's plumage, are also made from carotenoids, but apparently it takes a few extra internal physiological steps to obtain these. The equation that matters, though, is that a bird that is super-healthy is going to have capacity for doing this elite work as well as the normal processes of life. Red in the plumage is a visible sign of fitness. It so happens that birds have much more intense and discerning colour vision than humans do (they have three types of cones cells in the eye, not two), so they can probably assess a male's qualities a mile off.

It's a tough world out there for the male yellowhammer.

Eurasian nightjar

Caprimulgus europaeus

EURASIA; MIGRATES TO SOUTHERN PARTS OF AFRICA
FOR THE WINTER, 24–28 cm (9½–11 in)

 EVERY SUMMER, BIRDWATCHERS IN BRITAIN
perform a ritual. It involves going to listen to what
is possibly one of the strangest of all bird sounds
anywhere. They undertake this expedition on
some of the shortest nights of the year, often in
small parties of people who carry torches and put on insect repellent.
These parties leave their homes and journey to a special habitat
known as heathland, which is dominated by members of the heather
plant family; on a summer night these plants give off an almost sickly
aromatic scent. The people arrive at dusk, wander to a suitable spot
where it is open, but not far from woodland, and then wait in the
gathering darkness. The participants are not usually used to being out
in the wild at night, so there is a sense of excitement and possibility.
As it gets dark, the group revels in seeing the first stars and planets.

Sometimes an owl hoots early. There is often an initial flypast by another nocturnal bird, the woodcock, which is a long-billed, probing member of the snipe family that feeds on worms in damp patches of woodland. It flies over the treetops, offering a short gurgling croak followed by a loud 'SWISH!' as if a frog had been calling before unfortunately being stepped on.

As it finally gets truly dark, the moths begin to dance and the mosquitoes start to advance. Lights come on in the distance. There is a palpable tension. People fall silent, and everyone looks in all directions. Some people cup their ears. Who is going to hear it first? Almost invariably, somebody says excitedly that they are sure they can make out the sound, very much in the distance. Quietly, everybody thinks that they have jumped the gun.

But soon the waiting is over. The nightjar never starts loudly, with a flourish; its advertising call just tickles the ears softly, like a night-time breeze. If anything, it seems more as though somebody has flicked a modest switch to set off a mechanical device, something akin to a humming refrigerator. The nightjar's 'churr', as it is called, doesn't resemble any true bird song. It doesn't resemble an owl, or other night creature. The closest anybody seems to have got to a proper description is to liken it to a two-stroke motorcycle – the sort that everybody in southern Europe seems to drive at night on the narrow streets. There are

The nightjar never starts loudly, with a flourish; its advertising call just tickles the ears softly, like a night-time breeze.

two hollow reverberating tones, which alternate. The tones come from notes uttered at 25–42 to the second. And when the nightjar wishes to stop 'churring', its tremolo doesn't suddenly stop but just winds down, again like a faltering mechanical device.

Not surprisingly, the ancients tended to fear the strange call and, true to form, associated it with death and bad luck. A ridiculous legend grew up that the nightjar sucked the milk of goats and harmed them. You and I might chuckle at the absurdity, but the tale arose in several European cultures and persisted for centuries. It only goes to show how the night grows the imagination, and it takes many days of enlightenment to solve mysteries.

The nightjar's call might be a mechanical sound, but the flesh-and-blood reaction of the June-night explorers is almost always that of awe. The experience of hearing a wild nightjar is a strange one, and strangeness is always magnified by the disappearance of light and familiarity. It is an unusually deeply felt encounter. The nightjar-watchers' stumble home is always quieter and more reflective than their outward wander.

Eurasian skylark

Alauda arvensis

EURASIA, 18–19 cm (AROUND 7 in)

FOR THE LISTENER, ONE OF THE MANY delights of birdsong is that it is a blank canvas for our own emotions and experiences, which is no doubt one of the reasons why tuning in to the wild is now known to be good for our health (see page 34). As the listener, we can make of bird song what we will; in contrast to human music, so closely intertwined with composer and consumer, there are fewer and less strident human opinions to worry about. It is the bird and us. A corollary of this is that a bird song may evoke different emotions in different people – a nightingale, for example, is dramatic to some and peaceful to others.

There is one bird song, though, that seems to evoke almost exactly the same emotion in almost everybody who hears it within its western European range. It conjures up the zenith of summer, with warm sunshine and wafting breezes, its shrill outpourings as redolent of fair weather as the reassuring buzzing of insects. It is the skylark, yes, but really the 'summer-lark'.

It conjures up the zenith of summer, with warm sunshine and wafting breezes.

Listen to the song in isolation, perhaps a recording played on your smartphone, and it is perfectly acceptable. It is fast and shrill and cascading, a long monologue with subtle variations. But place it under the sun and it becomes ecstatic, indeed an exultation, with all the optimism and vigour of a fast-flowing stream – a stream of sound. The weather elevates the skylark's song into an experience.

This happens for several reasons. For one thing, the bird lives up to its name by singing in flight. It lifts off, fluttering, starting hesitantly, then gradually makes its way upwards into the air, performing as it goes. It may reach as high as 3om (98ft) up, hovering in an undulating manner. Once it reaches such heights, it is not so much singing as proclaiming. Those streams of sound cascade down like sweet saliva, refreshing all that they touch. After a couple of minutes, the bird begins an equally slow descent, still singing until, a metre or two from the ground, it plummets as if exhausted by its enterprise.

Another reason why skylarks are so dominant in the summer sun is that they don't perform alone. The males are strictly territorial, and their only way to lay claim to a patch of ground is to claim the air. This means that if a skylark hears a skylark, it literally rises to the challenge – the lark ascends. And that means, should you walk through the golden fields of high summer for any distance, you will not hear one lark, but many. One passes you on to another, and to another, a sort of air-traffic control.

The overwhelming delight of a summer-lark-time walk is far too much to have escaped Western poets, who converted the glorious songfest into enthusiastic verbiage. Take this offering, 'The Lark Ascending', from English Romantic poet George Meredith:

> *HE rises and begins to round,*
> *He drops the silver chain of sound*
> *Of many links without a break,*
> *In chirrup, whistle, slur and shake,*
> *All intervolv'd and spreading wide,*
> *Like water-dimples down a tide*
> *Where ripple ripple overcurls*
> *And eddy into eddy whirls;*
> *A press of hurried notes that run*
> *So fleet they scarce are more than one,*
> *Yet changingly the trills repeat*
> *And linger ringing while they fleet,*
> *Sweet to the quick o' the ear ...*

These delicious words inspired a still more famous composition of the same name, a beautiful orchestral work by English composer Ralph Vaughan Williams that has become one of Britain's favourite pieces of classical music. Ironically, this bird song, a wild gift, has given rise to music that obviously satisfies those strident opinions mentioned at the start of this essay.

You don't have to like the piece, or even the skylark itself, of course. That is part of its universal joy, its fanfare for everyone. But it is curious how the human experience can play tricks with reality – or at least, with the biology of the bird as a whole. We love the skylark for its song from aloft in summer. Yet curiously the skylark itself lives almost entirely on the ground and may be heard singing in every month of the year.

Northern cardinal

Cardinalis cardinalis

EASTERN AND SOUTHERN NORTH AMERICA, 20–25 cm (8–9 in)

IN THE CASE OF BIRDS, WE TEND TO ASSUME that the species with the best songs, such as the nightingale or the hermit thrush, are somewhat dowdy in plumage, the one compensating for the other, and often hidden away in thick foliage. And it is satisfying when the most beautiful birds have unremarkable voices. Take the tanagers, jewel-like stunners mainly found in South and Central America. To look at, they are beyond scintillating; but in every other way they are as dull as ditchwater.

It's just unfair when any being exudes unreasonable degrees of gorgeousness in seemingly every respect. But it happens. And around the world, there is perhaps no bird more richly endowed than the northern cardinal. You can appreciate its beauty on this page. The male's vermilion red is simply stunning and adorns most of its body.

The crest and black face simply set it off perfectly. And you can add popularity to its beauty. Cardinals are common birds in North America, regularly visiting bird feeders set up by adoring fans. The cardinal is the emblem of seven US states and is an icon.

The song, meanwhile, is a series of loud, sweet trills, together with whistles that slur somewhat deliciously up and down – 'Cheer, cheer, birdie, birdie, birdie ...'. It is incredibly pleasing, a bird song to drink a cocktail to. The cardinal has the excellent habit of singing almost throughout the year, so that it can enliven a day with glinting snow, or its notes can tickle as you slumber on a sultry afternoon. No wonder that the lucky Americans love it.

And should you be listening to a cardinal right now, in July, you might also bear witness to something remarkable. It is a truly intriguing moment of unusual intimacy between two birds, proof of a special partnership that might endear you to this bird even more.

The cardinal is unusual among temperate birds in that the female sings a lot – not as much as the male (about 10–20 per cent of the rate), but nevertheless far more

The cardinal has the excellent habit of singing almost throughout the year, so that it can enliven a day with glinting snow, or its notes can tickle as you slumber on a sultry afternoon.

than most. It sings, for example, to help protect the territory, which in the majority of small, non-tropical birds is the main task of the male, essentially alone. They also sing during conflicts with other females, and if the nest is threatened. The song of the female is no different to that of the male, so you cannot tell them apart by their sound.

What is truly remarkable about the female cardinal and its singing, though, is what happens when it is incubating eggs on the nest, or when it is brooding small young. At these times it sings frequently, and it seems that these songs are a code to the male, giving him messages about when to come with food and, presumably, when not to.

Consider these observations. In one study, when a male was within 12m (40ft) of the nest and made 'chip' calls, it would continue to visit the nest on 80 per cent of the occasions when the female responded with a song-phrase. If the female didn't sing in response to its calls, the male would stay away on half these occasions. The suggestion is that the female can limit a male's visits if required. After all, the male is a conspicuous and colourful bird; it is in both birds' interests not to give away the nest's location by visiting needlessly.

The code between male and female is even subtler than that, it seems. In another study, it was found that the female could give specific instructions to its mate. If a male sang nearby (within 12m) and she wanted it to deliver food, she would sing a different song type to the male (the male approached on 64 per cent of these encounters). If she didn't sing at all in response to his song-phrases, he would hesitate somewhat – and only make a visit on one in every three occasions. However, if the female matched his own song-phrase, this was apparently code for 'Keep away'. Only on 9 per cent of occasions that the female reflected his own song-phrase back to him did he approach – presumably to receive a well-deserved volley of abuse.

What a delightful thing to hear in your garden – a cardinal couple coordinating childcare. Can this bird be any more admirable? No wonder the Cherokee peoples used to summon up an incantation to imbue themselves with the spirit of this magical bird.

Common snipe

Gallinago gallinago

ACROSS NORTHERN EURASIA; MAY WINTER IN AFRICA,
INDIA OR SOUTHEAST ASIA, 25–27 cm (10–10½ in)

THE WORLD OF BIRDSONG HOLDS MANY surprises. And one of these is that not all songs are songs.

It's beyond midsummer, and up in temperate and especially Arctic Eurasia, the breeding season is in full swing. On boggy ground and wetlands, many shorebirds and waders are holding territories and nesting, and many of these make glorious advertising calls that cut across these open spaces and create a memorable atmosphere. One in particular is of great interest, though, sounding very different from the rest – the 'whinny' of the common snipe.

If you listen to this noise for the first time, especially if it's in the wild, it recalls the bleating of a sheep, and until you realize that it is coming from the air above you, and thus is unlikely to be the woolly ungulate, you might dismiss it as such. However, it is more plaintive than bleating, and much more rhythmic, buzzing and throbbing than a sheep's 'baa'. In English it is described as 'drumming'.

This is very much an advertising 'song', which serves to define and defend the territory of a common snipe. It's rarely, if ever, heard out of season, and it is part of a flight display that describes long circles and dives. Once the eggs hatch, it usually ceases altogether.

But it isn't a song, or a call. Or at least, it isn't a vocalization, as defined by something produced by the vocal tract. Remarkably, the whinny is produced by the sound of air moving past the feathers.

It isn't a vocalization, as defined by something produced by the vocal tract. Remarkably, the whinny is produced by the sound of air moving past the feathers.

If you are able to watch a snipe making the drumming, you might well notice that, as it does so, it spreads its tail so that the outermost feathers are fanned out away from the rest. It is the vibrating of these feathers that makes this remarkably far-carrying sound, which has been compared to that of a tethered flag in the wind.

Scientists put the outer tail feathers of museum specimens of snipe into a wind tunnel and discovered that the vibrations begin when the wind speed touches 24mph (39km/h). It was loudest at about double that, but any faster has the effect of destroying the feathers – so presumably the snipe itself has to make sure it isn't too exuberant! The sound frequency was measured at 350–400kHz but is heavily affected by harmonics. Fascinatingly, the next feathers in, towards the centre of the tail, did not produce the buzzing at all.

You might think that such a way to produce a song is brilliantly simple. You can make an impressive sound without opening your mouth; all you have to do is to fly high and dive down, and the work is done for you. However, drumming on its own rarely seems to be enough, because the snipe also has another territorial song made by the voice – a continuous, slightly hoarse 'chip ... chip ... chip ... chip'. This is usually made on the ground, but not always. Perhaps conditions aren't always right for the feather-song?

There is nothing quite like hearing a snipe drum. It is a real feature of wild places, and it is particularly heard at dusk, adding that extra something – often, you cannot see the bird at all. The rhythmic throbbing sounds otherworldly and strange; and that, of course, is exactly what it is.

Northern mockingbird

Mimus polyglottos

NORTH AMERICA AND WEST INDIES, 20–25 cm (8–10 in)

Now, in the moonlight, he sits here and sings.
A thrush is singing, then a thrasher, then a jay –
Then all at once, a cat begins meowing.
A mockingbird can sound like anything.

So writes Randall Jarrell, who was Poet Laureate of the United States in the 1950s. In his poem 'The Mockingbird' he describes one of America's most popular and iconic birds, and one of the most famous in the world. Possibly no other species apart from the lyrebird (see page 132) and the European starling (*Sturnus vulgaris*) are as celebrated for the curious quirk of mimicking the sounds of other birds and random sounds to include in their own utterances.

The moment you hear a mockingbird it gets your attention. You will hear a loud, well-enunciated phrase repeated several times, and then another phrase (or element) begins, also repeated until the singer switches to a different verse, again and again at a fast walking pace, the song bout seemingly incessant. The elements can be remarkably different – a trill there, a squeak next and a sweet warble following it. The mockingbird goes on and on; sometimes it repeats a sound it particularly likes over and over. But eventually it continues to the next. There seems no end to the bird's invention.

Perhaps there isn't. People have analyzed mockingbird repertoires and found that they vary, with some individuals including at least 250 elements. However, once scientists discovered this, they then found that a mockingbird keeps on improving its song as it grows older. (In avian life age is enormously valued; older, more experienced individuals almost invariably pair up before younger birds, or attract multiple mates. Ah, happy days!) More amazingly still, one study has found that the spring and autumn songs are almost completely different, suggesting that most repertoires have been underestimated by half!

And, of course, many but not all of the elements are imitations of other birds (as well as cats and so on, as mentioned by Jarrell). Among the most popular species imitated by mockingbirds are northern cardinals (see page 112), Carolina wrens (*Thryothorus ludovicianus*), tufted titmice (*Baeolophus bicolor*), blue jays (*Cyanocitta cristata*) and American robins (see page 44). It is intriguing to postulate how many of these imitations are direct copies of the birds in a mockingbird's home range, and which could be imitations stolen from other mockingbirds!

It is also the indefatigable quality of a mockingbird's song that sets it apart. It seems that an individual's mate is constantly monitoring the quality and variety of its song, and there is some evidence that, should a male not measure up to expectations, divorce will follow. Unmated males acutely underline their status by singing at night, as well as by day. They also sing and display more often than mated males, always in hope.

The liveliness and inventiveness of the mockingbird has long endeared it to humans. Native Americans believed that the mockingbird was present at the creation of the world, and as different tribes emerged, the bird itself handed out their new languages. Former US president Thomas Jefferson was one of many who kept several pet mockingbirds; in fact the species was a popular cage bird for a good 200 years. And, of course, it has found its way into a wealth of American literature. Here's another gem, this time from 19th-century poet Henry Wadsworth Longfellow in his poem 'Mocking-Bird':

Then from a neighboring ticket the mocking-bird, wildest of singers,
Swinging aloft on a willow spray that hung o'er the water,
Shook from his little throat such floods of delirious music,
That the whole air and the woods and the waves seemed silent to listen.
Plaintive at first were the tones and sad: then soaring to madness
Seemed they to follow or guide the revel of frenzied Bacchantes.

Why is the mockingbird so inventive and varied? It is, of course, a way of continually impressing your mate or your potential mate – a good repertoire is a sign of fitness.

But perhaps the question to ask is why does the mockingbird produce so much mimicry? Why not come up with its own phrases? One theory is that it could exclude the birds it mimics from its territory – although research so far suggests that the imitated birds aren't fooled.

The real reason is surely that mimicry is a fast track to improving what you are saying. Incorporating fresh voices spices up your composition. It's the very same reason I have incorporated quotations into this mockingbird musing.

Lawrence's thrush

Turdus lawrencii

SOUTH AMERICA, UPPER AMAZONIA, 20–23 cm (8–9 in)

IMAGINE YOU ARE A RESEARCHER, conducting a census of bird species in a forest in Upper Amazonia, perhaps for a conservation organization. Your task will be a laborious one. Simply walking around the locality, looking and listening from dawn to dusk will yield most of your species, but a lot will be missed if you have limited time. You can mist-net and catch more elusive species, but even then, such is the richness of this habitat that you are bound to overlook many that occur in the area. And you might survey at the wrong time of year. Some will be left out.

But it just so happens that there's an extra, most unusual method for surveying bird species in this part of the world, and that is to pay close attention to the local Lawrence's thrush. Easily overlooked, this mid-level and canopy species is an indefatigable singer. It performs all day, for hours at a time, with a few short breaks of about 15 minutes or so, as if it is undertaking a challenge for charity. It is also one of the world's greatest mimics. Mockingbird (see page 120), roll over – the Lawrence's thrush beats you hands down. It is a vocal sponge, mopping up fragments from all the forest sounds in its immediate vicinity – not just birds, but frogs and insects, too.

You might think that the above is a fanciful notion, but in fact it is a reality. On more than one occasion, the known range of a rare forest bird has been expanded because the call or song has been heard in the vocabulary of a Lawrence's thrush. The researchers knew to look for it and found it.

It is a vocal sponge, mopping up fragments from all the forest sounds in its immediate vicinity – not just birds, but frogs and insects, too.

The song of this sponge might not be what you expect. Many mimics, such as marsh warbler (page 184) and lyrebird (page 132) have a feverish delivery, but that of Lawrence's thrush is decidedly chilled. It sings a fragment and then leaves a good pause, which again is a researcher's dream, because it is so easy to make out every syllable. You have to listen for quite some time before you realize how varied it is: one moment there is the screech of a parrot, but later there might be the lowing of a ground-dwelling bird known as a tinamou. The fragments are all short, so a bird species with an elaborate song will be suitably abridged. It is all so effortless. And most of the time, you cannot even see the master imitator.

Over the years, the counts of imitations by individual birds have steadily risen. Back in the 1980s, scientists unveiled individuals that imitated 35 species and also included some phrases that were very much their own. The figure then rose to 51, and it now seems that some males can imitate 70 local species, including non-birds. A famous study conducted on the songs of 30 Lawrence's thrushes found that, in all, 173 species could be made out.

One of the truly odd things about this bird's exceptional mimicry is that none of its near relatives in the rainforests of Amazonia appear to have impressive songs at all. Why this particular species is quite so gifted is a mystery. It is thought, however, that Lawrence's thrush males probably compete for females using their repertoires and that the best birds probably mate with more than one female.

And therein lies an interesting thought. It could be that your avian survey is related to the quality of your thrush's repertoire. Before you analyze, perhaps it would be wise to see how many females your helper has attracted.

White bellbird

Procnias albus

NORTHERN SOUTH AMERICA, MAINLY GUIANA SHIELD,
27–28 cm (10½–11 in)

IN A BOOK ABOUT SONGBIRDS, IT WOULD BE a travesty to miss out the one with the loudest song of all. So, let me introduce you to the white bellbird. A pigeon-sized species that lives in tall forests in northern South America, it makes a loud, bell-like double 'klong-klang' that rings across the canopy. Amazingly, this call has been recorded at a sound of 125 decibels. That's about the same as a fire alarm, a loud rock concert, a turboprop plane taking off, or an industrial pile driver.

This call has been recorded at a sound of 125 decibels. That's about the same as a loud rock concert, a turboprop plane taking off, or an industrial pile driver.

The sound is rather like a very loud industrial klaxon, or a resonant hammer striking an anvil. It certainly isn't a 'normal' bird sound.

Indeed, the process of making the sound is also unusual. Before calling, the bird stoops down a little, then throws its whole body into the sound, as if exploding from within. The call is usually double, so the bird moves from one side to the other, its curious single, hanging wattle flopping over. In this species, the mouth is exceptionally wide, presumably to give maximum broadcasting potential. The ribcage is especially thick, and the abdominal muscles are particularly strong, presumably to stop the bird injuring itself when it calls. Internally, it also has a large syrinx, the organ responsible for bird sound.

The biggest mystery about the white bellbird's call is how it doesn't damage its own ears, and that of any potential mate, in the act of singing. The calls are so loud that if a person stood next to a bellbird (a little dangerous, since it is often 40m (130ft) up in the forest canopy), the effect would be extremely uncomfortable, and anyone would have to withdraw. The birds themselves must have some kind of protection, so far unknown.

But why does a white bellbird have such a loud voice? Well, it's sex, obviously. The act of being so noisy from a high perch is intrinsically risky, so it must benefit the genes. Seemingly, the females are attracted by the loudest voices.

For the females, selection is the easy part. The song carries for several kilometres, so it's no problem at all for the females to compare all the performers in the local vicinity without changing their perch. The males often coalesce into a relatively small area, just so that they're easily compared by potential mates.

The high perch of the white bellbird is its home base. It is likely to remain on it for almost 90 per cent of the daylight hours in the breeding season, calling intermittently. The vocalizing is its main daily activity. For a short time each day, it goes off to eat fruit. Fruit is so nutritious, and so ludicrously easy to find in the forest, that it doesn't take very long for a bird to have its fill, so after a few brief gulps, it's off to the singing post again. It is thought that many fruit-eating rainforest birds have evolved spectacular displays or extreme breeding behaviours, simply because their fruit diet absolves them from the daily grind of constant foraging.

For us, if we were fortunate enough to find ourselves in the northern South American forests, hearing a white bellbird cry would be the experience of a lifetime. Spare a thought for the other bird species that live nearby, though. The ear-splitting clanging must be the bane of their existence.

Superb lyrebird

Menura novaehollandiae

EASTERN AUSTRALIA, 76–103 cm (30–40½ in)

ABOUT NOW, EARLY SPRING IS BREAKING out in Australia. Along with the bushland flowers, one of the delights of the season is the peak song period for one of the continent's most iconic birds, the superb lyrebird. Males do sing all year round, but they are in full flow now, and it is perfectly possible to see them in action with snow lying on the ground.

The song of the lyrebird is so famous and celebrated that the eye-catching display is almost forgotten. The brown train of feathers, like that of a peacock that has lost its lustre, looks awkward as it trails along behind this strange, pheasant-like songbird. But in its moment, it is magnificent. While singing from a moderately raised perch, often a rock, the bird opens its tail like a fan, to reveal a net of whitish filamentous feathers and two elaborate broad outer feathers with serpentine striations and an elegant outward curve that resembles the arm of a lyre. These feathers are raised behind the singing bird like a curtain with two opulent cords, and sometimes they arch over the back almost as far as the head. It is quite a performance.

The accompanying song is proverbial in its power, intensity and variety, but what is truly special is its mimicry, which accounts for about three-quarters of the output. The copies it makes of common birds such as the laughing kookaburra (see page 148), eastern whipbird (*Psophodes olivaceus*), galah (*Eolophus roseicapilla*) and satin bowerbird (*Ptilonorhynchus violaceus*) are simply incredible – indeed, the lyrebird doesn't just copy one kookaburra, but can somehow manage a chorus of them. If you heard any in isolation, you would be completely fooled. But, of course, they all come during a bout of singing on the woodland floor. In a given location, about 25 per cent of all species find themselves being copied by the local lyrebirds.

While the mimicry of bush birds is impressive, it is perhaps the imitating of other sounds that has made the lyrebird a true megastar around the world. It frequently adopts Australian mammal sounds, such as that of the dingo and the koala, and in certain circumstances more bizarre sounds appear in

In a given location, about 25 per cent of all species find themselves being copied by the local lyrebirds.

its vocabulary. In the wild, these have included the creaking of a tree in the wind, and the wingbeats of birds, such as cockatoos, flying over. Yet a few individual lyrebirds, it seems, are even more inventive still. A bird in Adelaide Zoo became famous for imitating the noise of construction workers nearby, including hammering, sawing, running engines and, presumably, human swearwords. Others have been rumoured to mimic the sound of a camera motor drive.

Some of the best stories concern lyrebirds assimilating human shouts or other communications. One timber mill used to have a three-blast whistle to call staff to impromptu meetings, which the local lyrebird would apparently copy. It led to confusion and, one day, panic, when the bird issued the summons twice – the six-blast whistle was used as code for a fatal accident!

Some of these stories have an apocryphal whiff, and there's no doubt that very few lyrebirds copy peculiar human sounds. What is more intriguing is the way that the vocabularies are acquired and passed on from bird to bird. When lyrebirds were introduced to Tasmania (where they weren't native), the newly hatched offspring for some years tended to include only native mainland species in their song, some of which didn't occur on the island, proving that much of the repertoire is learned from other lyrebirds. Only over some considerable time were the calls of special Tasmanian birds incorporated. Most of the copies are transmitted culturally in the lyrebird population.

In that case, the possibility arises that a copy made hundreds of years ago could be issued by a contemporary lyrebird and passed down the generations. Maybe some lyrebirds give unrecognized calls such as now-extinct kangaroo species, or even the long-gone mainland population of the thylacine. Maybe the vanished thylacine is still with us in sound, resonating down the ages in the voice of a copyist.

Common wood pigeon

Columba palumbus

EUROPE, NORTH AFRICA AND WESTERN ASIA,
40–42 cm (AROUND 16 in)

IN THE ANNUAL WORLD OF BIRDSONG, THE cycle is on repeat. About now, the late summer forests in Europe resound to the coos of wood pigeons, just as they have year after year, decade after year,

for millennia. One of the many delights of the seasonal shifts in birdsong is that specific voices can be redolent of times, be they happy, sad or otherwise significant.

There is something earnest about the song of the wood pigeon, one of Europe's commonest birds. There are only five coos in its song

There are only five coos in its song sequence – a fast coo, two slow coos and finally another two quick ones – but they are delivered with great intensity and emphasis.

sequence – a fast coo, two slow coos and finally another two quick ones – but they are delivered with great intensity and emphasis, and if you watch the performer, it always gives maximum effort, its throat vibrating like an opera star. Yet the result is – well, just a few coos, isn't it? It's like a popular novel purporting to be great fiction. Many people listen to the simple dirge and laugh it off as a trivial part of the summer scene.

But as with some other birds, such as geese, there is glory in the collective. When pigeons coo in unison, something remarkable happens. It's often on a warm day, when the lower airspace is full of insects buzzing. Up in the sleepy canopy of the humming forest, the pigeons call all day long, coo upon coo, coo upon coo. The overall effect is like a soft mattress of sound, an incredibly peaceful, reassuring murmur. It's as if the heat has risen and is forming a bubble of simmering throatiness.

This peaceful, feelgood super-cooing must have been heard by our ancestors countless times, and perhaps on occasion some of them stopped to revel and bask in the zenith of summer. And we can still do so today, hundreds or thousands of years later.

Part of my own life's journey can be mapped out in the cooing of wood pigeons. Last summer, a chorus of these birds suddenly propelled me into a flashback. In an instant, transported by sound, I was standing next to an old house, sitting deep in the countryside near Bristol, England. It was a warm, sunlit day. I had long forgotten the moment, but the sound, the place and the atmosphere had an unmistakable authenticity.

It was a surprise to be back there, because my mind seems to have wiped out much of my early childhood. Or at least it has except for one day, the day my father departed from this life, when I was six years old. That day I can remember with vivid clarity, while much of the before and after is a blur. He died of a heart attack. He woke up that morning and never woke up again. My childhood vanished into a chasm of loss.

Well, I thought my boyhood memories had largely disappeared, but then came that curious flashback, so bright and fresh. It was from a moment a few weeks later, when my mother, sister and I had gone to stay with friends. Their old house was set in idyllic surroundings, far from London, where we lived. It must have given us breathing space from our tragedy, to wander in the woods. Who can imagine what my mother must have been going through, or my sister, of nine tender years, who witnessed my father passing away in front of her? As for me, all I can remember is the wood pigeons, that overwhelming cooing, that insistent declaring of high summer.

That flashback came from 50 high summers ago. Now I can appreciate what a traumatic time it was. Over the years, life has mollified the effect and I have received profound healing. But I have always been left with one terrible fear. Starting my own family and becoming a father, I struggled to shake off the terror of suddenly dying and leaving my daughter and son behind.

But each high summer the pigeons have cooed and, almost without noticing it, I have emerged through the key years of parenting unscathed, as babyhood led to school years and, latterly, university.

Many people are amused or annoyed when they hear a wood pigeon coo. But not me.

Streak-backed oriole

Icterus pustulatus

CENTRAL AMERICA, FROM NORTHERN MEXICO TO
COSTA RICA, 18–21 cm (7–8 in)

 OVER THE YEARS THAT BIRDSONG HAS BEEN
studied, it has become widely accepted that males
sing more than females. As far as the birds of north
temperate zones are concerned, females usually
sing hardly at all, and if they do, they use it in
exceptional circumstances. Those females that do sing regularly, such
as European robins (see page 156) or northern cardinals (page 112) tend
to do so much less often than males, and in some other species females
also make simpler utterances. In recent years, as more birds in the
tropics are being closely studied, there is evidence that pairs of various
species perform duets and that the females involved may sing as often,
or almost as often, as males.

However, it took a study of a slightly obscure Central American
bird to emancipate female birds fully. In the streak-backed oriole,

researchers finally showed that a female bird can indeed outperform a male, and by a wide margin. In this species, not only do females sing more often, but they also make phrases that are just as complex as those of the males. The song has been described as a series of rich whistles, sounding a bit like 'weechi-weechi-wee'.

The streak-backed oriole breeds as a solitary pair on the edge of a forest. It builds a pendulous basket for a nest, looking a little like a sock with a tennis ball in the toe. There is much competition for nest sites and also for nest material, with neighbours stealing from each other. As a result, both sexes defend the territory particularly strongly when breeding.

There is evidence that pairs of various species perform duets and that the females involved may sing as often, or almost as often, as males.

The oddest thing about the female's singing dominance is that, as well as defending the territory in concert with the male, she builds the nest entirely by herself, lays the eggs and is also responsible for all the incubation of the eggs. With so many tasks assigned exclusively to the female, you might expect the male to take the lion's share of territorial defence by singing, yet somehow it gets away with it. It does play an important role in feeding the young when they hatch, but after the breeding season, at about this time of year, the female again sings in defence of the territory, while the male goes almost quiet. This odd arrangement of breeding tasks seems very unfair and has yet to be fully explained.

There is another very intriguing quirk about the streak-backed oriole, which is again extremely unusual. The species occurs from northern Mexico south to Costa Rica. In the north of its range, close to the US border, the male's plumage is a great deal brighter than that of the female. However, as you go south this changes, and in Costa Rica the females are a good deal more colourful and look very similar to the males. So far, this hasn't been adequately explained either.

Since the song performance of female streak-backed orioles was discovered, a study of another obscure bird, the stripe-headed sparrow (*Peucaea ruficauda*) also reported that females sing more than males. This bird is also from warm parts of Central America. The likelihood is that, over time, more and more females will be proven to play an important or even key role in territorial defence by song.

We've come a long way from the long-held assumption that birdsong is largely a male preserve.

Eastern towhee

Pipilo erythrophthalmus

EASTERN NORTH AMERICA, 16–20 cm (6½–8 in)

MANY A NORTH AMERICAN BIRDWATCHER finds themselves grateful to the eastern towhee. Trying to learn birdsong holds terrors for many people as they attempt to disentangle the infamous jumble of similar voices that sound completely indistinguishable. But even the newest, greenest birder can pick up the essence of this common resident of edge habitats and scrub. Its loud call 'Tow-hee!' proclaims its name. Its most familiar song is an exuberant summons to 'Drink your tea-eeee!' and is completely unmistakable. Don't mind if I do!

Although you can readily identify the song, hidden within it are a wide range of variations. But the towhee's is the bird song that keeps on giving, and while the repertoires of many bird species are far too subtle for most of us to interpret, the variations in this species can be obvious even to an inexperienced listener. For example, a male might sing 'Drink-tea' instead, or 'Drink-tip', or perhaps 'Dri-i-ink your tea!' and sometimes just 'Your-tea'. Even the most inexperienced of birders cannot just identify the bird, but also appreciate two basic bird song facts: that individual birds often have more than one song-phrase; and that the songs of individual birds of the same species might differ from one another. Many people are completely unaware of both these things.

It is likely that the towhee provided a soundtrack to the fraught attempt to establish an English colony on the island of Roanoke, now North Carolina, back in the 16th century.

The variation in the song of the eastern towhee itself varies in a most intriguing way. In New Jersey, individual males sing an average of 4.5 songs, whereas in Florida, the average is eight. Nobody knows why this is the case.

Few people who enjoy the exuberant song of the eastern towhee are aware of the bird's connection to a tragic and mysterious event in the history of the USA. It is likely that the towhee provided a soundtrack to the fraught attempt to establish an English colony on the island of Roanoke, now North Carolina, back in the 16th century. We know that the settlers encountered the eastern towhee because one of the men involved in the initial attempt to settle the area was a certain John White, later Governor of the island. He spent a number of months there, from the summer of 1585 to the spring of 1586, and made a remarkable series of watercolours that depicted the local flora and fauna, as well as the life of the indigenous Americans of the local tribes, notably the Secotan. Among his paintings he depicted both male and female eastern towhees. These were the first images ever made of this species.

The second attempt to colonize Roanoke is the one steeped in intrigue and mystery. Settlers landed in 1587 and included John White's daughter Eleanor Dare, who soon gave birth to Virginia, the first English child born in a New World colony. The colonists struggled, so much so that John White was very quickly forced to return to England to gather extra supplies. His return was delayed by three years, and when he eventually returned to Roanoke in August 1590, all the colonists, a hundred or more people, had disappeared. To this day their fate has never been confirmed, although theories abound.

If you go to Roanoke island these days, you cannot avoid the trappings of tourism. You can find out how the settlers and Native Americans lived, you can visit the gift shops and you can be thoroughly immersed in the speculation about what happened to the Lost Colony. You can even get married there.

But how about an authentic experience? Go on to one of the nature trails and listen out for the distinctive song of the eastern towhee. You will then know for sure that you are sharing an experience with those settlers of 400 years ago.

Laughing kookaburra

Dacelo novaeguineae

EASTERN AUSTRALIA, 38–42 cm (15–16½ in)

SPRING IS GATHERING PACE IN AUSTRALIA right now, and on that ancient continent they do dawn choruses like nowhere else on Earth. While over most of the world the sweet voices hold sway, down under the dominant vocalists are loud, squawking, clarion-like and blunt. It's the most raucous dawn chorus on earth. In the country's largest city, Sydney, you are awoken by the carolling Australian magpie (see page 168), gurgling pied currawong (*Strepera graculina*) and grating channel-billed cuckoo (*Scythrops novaehollandiae*), which sounds like it's about to erupt; plus the screeching rainbow lorikeet (*Trichoglossus moluccanus*), sore-throated sulphur-crested cockatoo (*Cacatua galerita*) and Australian raven (*Corvus coronoides*), which sounds like a loudly complaining child (but check that these sounds aren't actually those of a loud, complaining child).

But preceding and often overriding these memorable voices, starting up while it is still dark, is the most famous bush alarm clock of all – the maniacal, bellowing laugh of the kookaburra. While it is quite possible to go to Australia and miss seeing some famous icons in the wild, such as koalas, emus and budgerigars, you would be hard-pressed not to encounter this fixture of parkland, suburbia, open woodland and bush. It is common over the eastern edge of the continent and has been introduced to the West, as well as to Tasmania and New Zealand.

People are often amazed to find out that the kookaburra is a member of the kingfisher family. In Europe, the native kingfisher is the 'dash, flash and splash' bird, a jewel in a hurry that zips fast and away low over rivers; in North America, the belted kingfisher (*Megaceryle alcyon*) is bigger and brasher than that, but hardly a distinguished vocalist. The kookaburra breaks the kingfisher mould – it is a dry country bird, and instead of fish, it eats lizards, small mammals and anything that cannot run away in time.

The famous advertising call is quite complex, consisting of five parts, which in order are: the 'kooa', the 'cackle', the 'rolling', the 'ha-ha' (that's the laugh, in case you wondered) and a final element, which can either be the 'gogo' or the 'gurgle'. The 'gogo' indicates that the vocalist is a male, and the 'gurgle' is made by the female, so if you listen carefully, you can tell. Mind you, the birds often loudly duet; they do this with all the expertise of tone-deaf members of an amateur theatre group doing *Carmen*, so they often talk over each other and you cannot hear the final elements in the cacophony. Sometimes kookaburras live in small groups, in which case everybody takes part, and it is even harder to tell which individuals are which.

The kookaburra was never going to be one of the overlooked members of the Australian avifauna; a brown thornbill (*Acanthiza pusilla*) it is not. Naturally, it has played a predominant role in

Aboriginal culture, a feature no less of their creation story. According to tradition, when the gods had made day and night, they appointed the kookaburra to be the sentinel of daybreak, awakening humans and animals alike.

It has played a role in more recent Australian culture, too, of course – and indeed well beyond. It has always been a great favourite in its native land, because its fearlessness and confidence chimes with the perceived national character. During the First World War, people would send postcards of a mocked-up kookaburra in military uniform to those serving in Europe as a symbol of good luck. The bird still appears on souvenir shop gifts, and the name is used for commercial companies and much else. It's also the subject of a popular 1930s nursery rhyme:

Kookaburra sits in the old gum tree,
Merry, merry king of the bush is he.
Laugh, Kookaburra, laugh, Kookaburra
Gay your life must be!

Another place where the kookaburra crops up in popular culture is as a soundtrack in movies, invariably to emphasize the jungle, which ironically is not its natural habitat at all. The most famous appearances, even remembered today, were in the highly influential *Tarzan* films of 1932–48. These were set in Africa but featured a laughably incorrect mix of wildlife from all parts of the world. Kookaburras laughing often followed elephants trumpeting, macaws from South America screeching, and then Johnny Weissmuller's fantastic ululating yell. The films were much loved and nobody ever seemed to care.

African fish-eagle

Haliaeetus vocifer

SUB-SAHARAN AFRICA, 64–75 cm (25–29½ in)

THE BIRDS OF PREY ARE SPECTACULAR and exciting, dominant in our cultures and in our imagination, and so it is surprising that their calls are not generally very well-known. However, there is a reason for this: on the whole, raptor vocalizations aren't up to much. They are often infrequent and unexpectedly quiet. They don't vary much, either. A few squawks and whistles are usually the pattern, and these often sound breathy and feeble.

There are a few exceptions, though, and one of the very best is that of the African fish-eagle. It has been declared 'the sound of Africa', although one suspects that such a name arose from swapping safari tales in fancy restaurants after a little too much bourbon. It is, nonetheless, loud and far-carrying and extremely persistent. If you spend a whole day beside any large sub-Saharan African wetland, be it a marsh, lake or river, then you might go to bed with the call ringing in your inner soundtrack.

The call is a loud, shrill yelping, quite similar to the yelp of a puppy. It is uttered in a series, with an introductory yelp followed by a sort of triple echo: 'Wee-ah, hio-hio-hio'. It is frequently uttered as a duet, in which the male has a higher-pitched (treble) voice and the larger female a lower contralto. It is usually the female that begins a duet. When they call, both sexes throw their head back, adding some extra dramatic effect.

The birds start calling at dawn, then at times throughout the day and in many social situations; they don't seem to need much encouragement. For example, a bird distantly flying over might be enough to provoke a reaction, and maybe just an unrelated disturbance. If they were modern-day humans, they would presumably perform their exclamatory ceremony when an email came in.

It is frequently uttered as a duet, in which the male has a higher-pitched (treble) voice and the larger female a lower contralto.

The process of calling is serious stuff, however, because African fish-eagles are highly territorial. On a given day they will spend about 80 per cent of their time at home, just hanging around, usually perched on the top of waterside trees, often dead ones. If their patch is threatened, though, their mood instantly changes and they will routinely physically fight any rivals, real or imagined. It is, of course, all about resources.

As their common name implies, African fish-eagles are piscivorous, although they will routinely switch their predatory instincts towards birds (such as flamingos at soda lakes), monkeys, frogs and, occasionally, young crocodiles. The feeding method is to watch from their elevated perch, and then swoop down to snatch a fish from the surface of the water below. The prey is gripped in the talons and carried off or, if it is too heavy to be handled this way, the bird uses its wings to 'row' ashore.

One very poorly appreciated aspect of bird of prey biology, which applies to almost all species, is their strong tendency towards piracy. Catching live prey requires enormous effort, cunning, planning and good luck – prey animals are reluctant to be caught and eaten, after all. Therefore, if a bird of prey sees another one that has been successful, it instantly senses an opportunity. A significant percentage of food consumed by icons such as the peregrine (*Falco peregrinus*) or bald eagle (*Haliaeetus leucocephalus*) is stolen from another hunter. The African fish-eagle is especially prone to this because its food is taken by many other bird species, so it frequently terrorizes birds such as herons and storks, pelicans and the western osprey (*Pandion haliaetus*), either attacking them or harassing them until they give up their meal. These enormous birds will even steal from kingfishers, which does seem pretty poor form.

Perhaps that famous call should be described slightly differently – a yelp followed by a chuckle, perhaps?

European robin

Erithacus rubecula

EUROPE, NORTH AFRICA AND WESTERN ASIA, 14 cm (5½ in)

I LIKE TO AMUSE PEOPLE AT THIS TIME of the year by giving them some British bird song advice. Go into the woods any time now, in September, with some gullible friends. Then listen for the sound of any bird whatsoever that is making a proper song, with sentences and structure, as opposed to a monosyllabic call note (see page 9), and declare that the singer is a robin. Your friends will be duly impressed and, unless you are unlucky enough to have picked up the occasional phrase from a Eurasian wren, you will also be absolutely right.

September is the time when, after a summer truce when birds have been bringing up young and then moulting, European robins resume their tendency towards territorial violence. These small birds, objects of enormous affection among the British in particular, are nonetheless exceptionally aggressive. A study long ago found that as many as 10 per cent of the males in a robin population succumbed to fights with their own species. These fights are not pretty. They often involve a quick grapple and then a sharp peck towards the delicate forehead of the opponent, causing instant death and a sad pile of brown and orange feathers.

However, a robin's lifestyle means that the ownership of a territory is paramount for its survival. These small birds need space; they usually hunt from an elevated perch, waiting for an invertebrate to wander into view, and it really doesn't help if they are disturbed. So, it is imperative for an individual to fight for its own patch, and to hell with the competition. The skirmishes start now. And to complicate the situation, not only are the young of the year fighting for space, so are the female robins. Borders will be reduced; tempers will be hotter.

You would never know that your local robins were under pressure, such is the relaxed, silvery nature of their song. They sing a phrase and then pause before the next one, which is always different from the last. The phrases have a definite stop-start quality, with some rapid sections and others much slower, but overall the delivery is distinctly in league with the season – mellow, if fruity. It is said that, in comparison with the spring song, the autumn delivery has a more melancholic mien, but that could merely match the mood of the listener. It is also supposed that the phrases are somewhat longer.

You have plenty of time to make up your mind about this, because the song of the robin will be our constant companion from now into the very depths of winter. Each autumn morning, robins will dominate the European bird chorus, but they will perhaps be appreciated most in the evenings, when these birds will often sing in the gloaming, the long and depressing fall of night. Fitted with unusually large eyes, which are adapted for feeding in the shade of forests, robins are highly sensitive to light and readily sing, even in the middle of the night, when streetlights are on. As far as humanity is concerned, the robin is a bird that keeps on giving.

Winter-evening robins are often supposed to be nightingales by the general public, who assume that anything that sings in the darkness is the famous bird. However, nightingales are summer visitors to Europe and have a short singing season between April and June (see page 63). The birds are very closely related, but with divergent lifestyles.

Each autumn morning, robins will dominate the European bird chorus, but they will perhaps be appreciated most in the evenings, when these birds will often sing in the gloaming.

The tendency of robins to sing in reaction to streetlights appears to have a knock-on effect on their lifestyle. A recent study found that robins with territories that were in areas with a lot of artificial light were less zealous in defence of their territory than nearby birds exposed to more natural conditions. These birds reacted less to the stimulus of a stuffed rival. Such robins expend less energy defending these well-lit patches, suggesting that their territories are of lower quality and less worth fighting over. The best birds stayed in the dark.

Another interesting piece of research found that robins in urban areas tended to sing more at night. But this wasn't because of the lights; it was because of the noise. The streets were quieter at night, allowing the birds to make themselves heard.

It's clearly not easy, living close to humankind!

Regent honeyeater

Anthochaera phrygia

EASTERN AUSTRALIA, 20–23 cm (8–9 in)

I'VE TRIED TO AVOID THE SUBJECT UNTIL now. This book is a celebration of birdsong and hopefully it lifts the spirits. But sooner or later, we have to accept that we have a fractured, plundered, altered world, and the main problem is that humans have not always been good at looking after nature. Almost every bird species has been affected by humans in some way, whether it be reducing habitat, direct persecution or disturbance. And the human world even impinges on birdsong, that purest of wild gifts.

Take the case of Australia's regent honeyeater. In every way, this bird is a stunner, with its spangled plumage and brilliant yellow on the wings and tail, which suggest that it catches fire as soon as it flies. Medium-sized, it has a very Australian habit of moving about from place to place, unpredictable and nomadic. It feeds on the nectar of eastern Australia's eucalyptus heaven, along with its attendant bugs. It is loosely sociable, especially in the non-breeding season, when it commonly associates with some closely related honeyeaters such as wattlebirds and friarbirds. These flocks join in a very loud and thrilling communal chorus, like an excited audience waiting to hear a concert, which never starts! During these times, young regent honeyeaters pick up some of the calls of their relatives and adopt mimicry into their songs.

Young regent honeyeaters pick up some of the calls of their relatives and adopt mimicry into their songs.

However, most of the song that a young male regent honeyeater adopts is learned much earlier in life, from the father and other older males in the same breeding vicinity; regent honeyeaters can be informally colonial. The result is a pleasing series of liquid, rolling notes squeezed into a babble, with great variety. It is a difficult song to describe; it is neither bad nor outstanding. It serves its purpose, helping to attract females and keep territory.

The regent honeyeater was once quite a common bird over large parts of south-east Australia, even occurring in the suburbs of Sydney and Melbourne. Flocks of thousands were occasionally reported. However, since the 1940s, it is estimated that 75 per cent of its former eucalyptus-rich habitat has been destroyed or degraded. This sort of problem has affected many Australian birds, but for reasons that aren't entirely clear, this species has fared much worse than most. It has long gone from South Australia and declined to a catastrophic level. It is possible that now, in the early 2020s, there may be only 300 birds left in the wild.

One of the biggest problems facing the regent honeyeater now is that its populations are fragmented. There are a few refuges with modest numbers, but widely scattered, and the birds' nomadic tendencies disperse them further. It is obvious that this is a problem for the regent's breeding in the wild. Boy needs to meet girl across a crowded eucalyptus habitat, not a scattered range.

There is a subtler problem, too: male regent honeyeaters are beginning to lose their lustre to prospective females, and it is because they are no longer learning to sing properly. It isn't their fault; the males simply don't have enough tutors in the wild to help them perfect their song.

And it gets worse. With so few of their kind left, the honeyeaters are mimicking too many songs of other birds. It's all very well singing your imitation of a friarbird to the girl of your dreams, but she also wants to know who you really are. She wants to hear the regent within. But if there isn't enough of your authentic voice, it could spell disaster.

It has become so serious that conservationists in Australia have begun to step in. Scientists of the Taronga Conservation Society have taken to rearing regent honeyeaters in captivity and literally playing sound recordings of multiple males to the chicks, as well as housing them within hearing distance of other captive birds. A brief study has found that, once released back into the wild, the tutoring gives them a slightly enhanced chance of survival to breed.

It's a delightful conservation story, but then you begin to contemplate what has made it necessary. Parts of our world are so broken that birds cannot learn to sing properly. What a terrible mess we are making.

Musician wren

Cyphorhinus arada

LOWLAND NORTHERN SOUTH AMERICA, INCLUDING THE
AMAZON BASIN, 12 cm (AROUND 5 in)

IT ISN'T OFTEN THAT BIRDSONG MAKES YOU laugh because, to be honest, it isn't funny. The odd bird, such as the great bustard (*Otis tarda*) makes noises that resemble embarrassing human bodily functions, and it's fun to hear parrots imitating humans swearing, or a trained bullfinch (*Pyrrhula pyrrhula*) whistling the German national anthem. But on the whole, unless you're talking about owls, bird vocalizations aren't a hoot.

But some do reach beyond the realm of marvellous and well into 'amazing' and 'delightful' territory, which might make us chuckle in sheer wonder. And one of these is the aptly named musician wren, a true bird of the Amazon jungle. Listen and you will be beguiled.

The wren family is famous for its members' vocal prowess. The Eurasian wren (*Troglodytes troglodytes*) is celebrated for its complexity and its vehemence; its oft-repeated phrase can sound like an enthusiastic sports commentator accelerating to the conclusion of a hundred-metre race, always at risk of tripping over words. The spritely trill of the house wren (*T. aedon*), which sounds as though you have opened your purse and coins have spilled out, is a fixture of wild tracks for movies. The variety of wren sounds is astonishing, and some of their common names are distinctive, too: how about happy wren (*Pheugopedius felix*), nightingale wren (*Microcerculus philomela*), flutist wren (*M. ustulatus*) and song wren (*Cyphorhinus phaeocephalus*)?

The musician wren is the most entertaining of the lot. Its song is sort of a jingle of beautifully clear whistles, which jump up and down in pitch as if written by an inept composer, interspersed with odd, slightly gurgling notes. The tones are quite organ-like (this species is occasionally known as the organ wren), so perhaps the best way to describe the song is that it sounds like a child sitting down and pretending to play the organ, and every so often shifting in their seat.

The bird itself lives in the understorey of rainforest and lives in pairs. In common with several other species of tropical wrens, it will commonly sing in duet, or at least antiphonally, one bird singing and the other responding. Several other forest wrens sing very tightly coordinated duets, in which it is almost impossible to tell which bird is doing which section, unless you are standing between them. These duets are often begun by a female, with the male joining in to establish that the pair bond is strong between the two. Musician wrens don't seem to be quite so focused on the duet.

In Brazil, hearing musician wrens is supposed to bring you good luck, although if you are already birdwatching in the Amazon rainforest, then you have already been showered with luck and probably don't need any more. There is also a legend that as soon as the musician wren starts singing, everything else in the forest stops to listen. It is nonsense of course – the only animals to do so would be human beings, captured by wonder.

Australian magpie

Gymnorhina tibicen

AUSTRALIA AND NEW GUINEA; INTRODUCED TO FIJI AND
NEW ZEALAND, 37–43 cm (14½–17 in)

HOW DO YOU DESCRIBE THE INDESCRIBABLE?
I have frequently written about Australian magpies,
and the point always comes when you have to put
their astonishing sounds down in words. There you
flail. But you still try. Invariably there will be words
such as yodelling and carolling, fluting (the scientific name *tibicen*
means 'flautist') and gargling. But none of those terms, while useful,
does any justice to the reality. If you bear in mind that the best-known
memory phrase in Australia is 'Quardle oodle ardle waddle doodle',
then perhaps you'd do better never to try. All you can do is listen to an
Australian magpie recording and be transfixed.

One of Australia's most widespread and common birds, the magpie,
named after its black-and-white plumage like the European bird, but
no relation, is also one of the noisiest. Pairs and groups hold territory

year-round, and they sing year-round at any time of day or night. They have dawn songs, dusk songs and even their own night song – their special moonlight cantata. Most species of birds prefer to sing while perched in a tree, but magpies will spontaneously burst into song anywhere, even on the ground. They're impossible to ignore. On that continent, you are never more than a few hundred metres away from a singing Australian magpie.

They have dawn songs, dusk songs and even their own night song – their special moonlight cantata.

Not surprisingly, this character is one of the best known of all Australian birds. It completely invades human spaces and, as a result, helps to define the soundscape of suburbia. The birds sometimes live in pairs, but more often exist in groups of varying size; sometimes just the pair plus their most recent progeny, sometimes a group of adults and youngsters. Within any system, every so often a senior bird starts gurgling, and seconds later the rest of the group join in, resulting in one of the endless cacophonies. There seem to be various functions of these communal ramblings. They are used for territorial defence at a distance, during actual skirmishes, as a celebration of flock togetherness and sometimes simply to signal that a good source of food has been unearthed. These crow-sized birds are carnivorous, eating insects, spiders, small birds, and mammals, such as mice, lizards and frogs. They also take dead meat, such as roadkill.

Despite the fact that Australian magpies are impossible to ignore and are ubiquitous, even in towns and cities, there are not many people who would admit to feeling much affection for them. The reason for this is that, during the midst of the breeding season (about now), they are extremely aggressive in defence of their territory. This means challenging allcomers – other birds, goannas, snakes, dogs and, of course, people. They seem to have a particular dislike of cyclists, setting on them vigorously and

It completely invades human spaces and, as a result, helps to define the soundscape of suburbia.

quite frequently causing accidents; sometimes these have been known to have fatal consequences. Pedestrians, especially children, are sometimes injured when aggressive magpies peck at their faces, and both people and livestock have been known to lose the sight of an eye. Of course, rather like shark attacks, the genuine harm done by rogue individuals is very much the exception rather than the rule. Nonetheless, once gatherings of human Australians have exhausted their usual topics of conversation, everybody has their 'magpie story' to tell.

One solution to Australia's magpie problem, which has proven particularly popular with schoolchildren, is to wear a large, wide-brimmed hat with a pair of scary-looking eyes painted on the back. There is absolutely no proof that this works at all, but it makes a great Australian souvenir – perhaps more authentic than a hat hung with corks.

Hwamei

Garrulax canorus

CHINA, LAOS AND VIETNAM, 21–24 cm (8¼–9½ in)

YOU WOULDN'T WANT TO MESS WITH A hwamei. Why else would there be a strange old Chinese tradition that heavies, henchmen and other undesirables would go about carrying this attractive singing bird in a cage in front of them? It was apparently their calling card. Instead of knuckle-dusters or knives, they would carry elaborate cages on a stick to set out their aggressive stall, and the rest of the respectable population of the south Yangtze would cower. This tradition carried on until the early 20th century.

It could only be because of this character's reputation as a street fighter, albeit a golden-voiced one. The hwamei has a gorgeous song, one of the finest in Asia, composed of slurred whistles, ringing notes and warbles, and almost any other melodious word you can use. It characteristically often starts slowly, but gets better and better as the phrase goes, and it also rises in pitch. It's euphonious, but the singer is among the most viciously territorial of birds, a behavioural version of the cute-looking but red-bloodied, sometimes murderous European robin (see page 156). It is so combustible that bird catchers in China, who are always on the lookout for the best singers of the district, simply use a cage with two compartments – one for a captive bird, one adjacent – and a trapdoor, to catch one. The male hwameis only have to hear the song and the red mist descends. They must see the cage, but they cannot help themselves. They keep their pride but lose their freedom.

The hwamei has a gorgeous song, one of the finest in Asia, composed of slurred whistles, ringing notes and warbles, and almost any other melodious word you can use.

All over Asia, hwameis are popular contestants in cage-bird contests, which still thrive today, and often attract wide audiences and big prizes. One of the main centres of competition is Singapore. Here, bird-singing contests are followed with such fervour that alongside them has literally sprung up what must be one of the most niche cottage industries in the world. Apparently, a diet of grasshoppers is a song stimulant, so a small number of enterprising folk have made themselves into self-employed grasshopper catchers.

This bird, incidentally, is a member of a bird family known as the babblers. They are chiefly forest birds of Asia, with small numbers in Africa, and they often keep themselves to themselves in the undergrowth. What is remarkable is that there are about 300 species, and they include some of the most utterly gorgeous birds in the Oriental region, with bold colours and markings, and often sweet voices.

The interest in the hwamei, the most famous member of the family, has fortunately not yet resulted in any serious dent in the bird's wild population. This is probably largely because it isn't a bird of true forest, but rather of scrub and second growth. Its range and abundance seem to be holding up well for now. In Hong Kong, China, where trapping is now discouraged, it is holding its own.

However, no wild bird can sustain trapping above a certain level, and there is a danger that this could be reached in the near future. It would be truly sad to leave the hwamei's population in a mess.

Tawny owl

Strix aluco

EUROPE AND WESTERN ASIA, 37–38 cm (14½–15 in)

IN THE NORTHERN HEMISPHERE THE nights are drawing in. The reality of autumn and the certainty of winter are gripping. In the wild, after a late summer truce, birds are beginning to become territorial once again, and nowhere is this territoriality noisier, or more extreme, than in the woods after dark.

For bird enthusiasts, the nocturnal chorus of hooting tawny owls is fantastic. There are few more atmospheric bird sounds anywhere. It is so evocative and haunting that the creative industries have routinely used it to unsettle the viewer of a movie or TV drama, tapping into our universal, deep-rooted fear of the night. In the early years of Hollywood, many hoots of this strictly Eurasian owl found their way on to the wild tracks of American films.

In Western literature, there are multiple references to owls as reflecting life's shadowy, sinister side. The tawny owl's scientific name *Strix* is Greek for 'witch,' and the connotations are not complimentary. The famous witches' brew stirred in William Shakespeare's *Macbeth* included a 'howlet's wing'. For hundreds of years, wherever tawny owls have lived alongside people they have been associated with mischief or bad luck, and frequently both. For example, it was widely believed that if an owl flew past the window of a sick person's room, their death was imminent. Dead owls were sometimes nailed to doors to ward off evil. Encounters were fraught with fear and suspicion. Take this from the 19th-century English poet Edward Thomas:

An owl's cry, a most melancholy cry
Shaken out long and clear upon the hill,
No merry note, nor cause of merriment.

The main territorial hoot consists of an initial, short semi-hoot, followed by a long gap of at least four seconds and then another introductory hoot preceding a longer, quavering one. Sometimes hoots are uttered in isolation. The deep tone and the quavering are characteristically melancholy, even tragic in nature, which partly explains why they send shivers down your spine. The current hooting matches in the crisp autumn air do in fact have tragic undertones. They are sharply unfriendly towards any listening rivals, warning them to keep off inhabited territory. Any bird that tries to infringe the borders is dealt with ruthlessly; these hoots are made for thwarting.

This uncompromising message is aimed at allcomers, even a tawny owl's youngsters, which an adult will kill if it is deemed necessary. It seems an odd waste of effort, since tawny owls start breeding early and will look after their young for as long as 80 days after the latter have left the nest, feeding them, keeping them safe and tutoring them in hunting. But in the autumn the young become a liability and must move on; they must not upset the fragile goodwill of their parents.

That's because a tawny owl's territory is its world. Once it is settled in, an owl will remain at home until death. Over the months and years, it gets to know its patch intimately; where to hunt, when and in what weather; where food is reliable, and so on. Any threat to its routine is met with necessary force.

So, the haunting hooting is a warning, the chorus is a conversation of challenges set and repelled. It is no friendlier than, perhaps, it sounds.

The tawny owl is the subject of one of the oldest misinterpretations of a bird sound in the Western world. Written in the early 1590s, another of Shakespeare's plays, *Love's Labour's Lost* includes the following lines as it draws to a close:

Then nightly sings the staring owl:
Tu-who;
Tu-whit, to-who – a merry note,
While greasy Joan doth keel the pot.

Ornithologists down the years have pointed out that the tawny owl doesn't actually sing in this way at all. The 'To-who' calls are the hoots of a male, and they are typically heard in isolation. Meanwhile, the 'Tu-whit' sounds very like the call of both sexes, which is a sharp 'ke-wick'. What Shakespeare describes is likely a duet by a male and a female, not the nightly song of a single bird. Nobody really cares, of course, and besides, any correction would be more than 400 years too late.

It is, though, an apt irony that Shakespeare's description of what we are hearing now in the autumnal gloom should be from *Love's Labour's Lost*. If ever there were a title for the searing break in the bond between parent and young owl, it would surely be this.

Coppersmith barbet

Psilopogon haemacephalus

INDIAN SUBCONTINENT, SOUTHEAST ASIA AND
THE PHILIPPINES, 15–17 cm (AROUND 6 in)

IT IS WELL KNOWN THAT FROGS CALL AT a higher rate when the temperature rises and their own body heat increases. Could there be an equivalent in birds? At first it seems unlikely, since birds are warm-blooded, but how about the coppersmith barbet, a small but chunky bird that is a distant relative of the woodpeckers? It has been reported that as the summer heats up in India, so the calling of the barbet increases in rate. Apparently, this species can call at anything between 80 and 200 times a minute. What if there was an equation that allowed you determine the one from the other? Recording the temperature is just about the only thing a smartphone cannot do, so perhaps you could attach an app to tap into the local barbets and work it out?

The coppersmith barbet isn't a songbird, and its advertising calls are potentially among the most monotonous on Earth. The sound is simply a repetition of 'tok', on and on and on. It has been likened to time-signal pips, or to the repetitive sound of moving machinery in a factory. Originally named after the sound made by a metalworker, it ought to be one of those noises that would ordinarily drive everybody mad.

Yet there is something different about the advertising call that mollifies the monotony, and that's probably that it is a classic background sound. It is never too loud, and in no way discordant. Go to rural India and it is a familiar noise in communities, remarkably unobtrusive against the usual chickens, people shouting, scooters, and car horns. You can hear it as you go about your business, walking, driving or cycling; indeed, it is perfectly possible to hear the 'tok, tok' from inside a tuk-tuk. Like a blackbird in a city in Europe, or a robin in North America, it provides a small nudge that there's a wild environment beyond the bustling human one. It is just a reminder, a back-of-the-minder, an outside-the-grinder. You fancy that if the human race were to destroy itself, its empty Asian communities would still resonate to the avian 'tok'-ing clock.

In common with a blackbird in a city in Europe, or a robin in North America, it provides a small nudge that there's a wild environment beyond the bustling human one.

It is mainly, but not exclusively, the male that advertises; sometimes the pair sing over each other's voices. The vocalist invariably turns its body around as it does so, one moment broadcasting in one direction and the next, a different one. This means that the barbet can be difficult to locate, which presumably is the intention, as it often broadcasts from high in a tree, often on a dead snag.

And if you want to know a place where you're guaranteed to see barbets, as well as lots of forest birds, find a fig tree with ripening fruits! Barbets have a broad diet, but what they enjoy more than anything else are figs, which they eat in great quantities. In the tropics, a fig bounty is one of the great treats of the birding world, since it attracts birds (and mammal) from a wide area and there's a palpable sense of excitement.

If barbets had smartphones, there would be a fig-finder.

Marsh warbler

Acrocephalus palustris

EUROPE; WINTERS IN EASTERN AND SOUTHERN AFRICA, 13 cm (5 in)

IF EVER THERE WERE A BIRD SONG THAT typified the lushness and fertility of central Europe in midsummer, it would have to be that of the marsh warbler. One of the very latest species to arrive in the north after its long migration from tropical Africa, the marsh warbler often pitches up in June and sings the days and nights away with a demented fervour. Its crazy song is the icing on the dawn chorus cake for those on the Continent, that last and maddest piece of the midsummer babble.

So why, you might ask, is it this week's bird, as the days sink in the northern hemisphere and winter grips? Well, it isn't as though the marsh warbler has disappeared – it has just become an African bird once again. This transcontinental migrant spends the winter towards the southern and eastern part of Africa, and spends longer here than it ever does on its breeding grounds. You could argue that it's an African bird that happens to go north to reproduce.

But there is a specific reason for including the marsh warbler now, and it's a remarkable one. It's because young marsh warblers are, at this moment, still learning their songs. Why is this important? Because the marsh warbler is exceptionally unusual among all the world's birds for having a song that is probably 100 per cent mimetic. In other words, every syllable of its song is borrowed, copied from whatever sounds the young bird picks up from its environment.

Quite a few species are mimetic, as we know. The northern mockingbird (see page 120) and the superb lyrebird (page 132) are good examples, incorporating multiple plagiarism into their songs. But what differentiates the marsh warbler is that it not only picks up sounds in its breeding areas, but also in tropical Africa where it winters. The young marsh warbler is known to be sensitive to learning new fragments of song for the first eight months of its life, which means that, say, if it hatches in July, it will still be learning in March or April. The song is completed by its first breeding season. But right now, it is absorbing African bird songs into the mix.

The marsh warbler is unusual among all the world's birds for having a song that is probably 100 per cent mimetic.

Hearing a marsh warbler, you would never know that all its elements are borrowed, so seamlessly do they fit into its lively, liquid, continuous chatter, which includes superbly manic asides and frenzied ramblings. Many motifs are repeated a few times in succession, but you can never predict what might come next – and who knows if the bird itself does, as it jams and improvises? It would be a fantastic song even without the intrigue of its imitations.

A few years ago, the brilliant Belgian ornithologist Françoise Dowsett-Lemaire studied recordings of marsh warblers to evaluate what and how many species from both continents were copied in each bird's song. Her results were extraordinary. Thirty birds singing from Belgian edges and marshes were found to sing fragments from 99 European species and 113 African species, the latter including doves, hornbills and some tricky brown warbler-like birds called cisticolas. In fact, some of the African birds were so localized that she could narrow down exactly where the migrants had been.

On average, each individual marsh warbler imitated 76 different species of birds. And, again on average, 45 of these came from Africa and 31 from Europe. This could reflect the relative amounts of time spent learning sounds from each area, or perhaps tells of the much greater richness of species in tropical Africa. It is impossible to say.

Evaluating recordings of marsh warblers and identifying not just European bird songs from them but also those from a huge region of Africa takes the most formidable experience and skill and, not surprisingly, nobody has yet added to Dowsett-Lemaire's work. It is also possible that some other more occasionally imitative long-distance migrants, such as the reed warbler (*Acrocephalus scirpaceus*), sedge warbler (*A. schoenobaenus*) and Blyth's reed warbler (*A. dumetorum*) might do something similar.

In the meantime, we can be grateful for a wondrous discovery – that a small bird is learning tropical sounds right now that in a few months' time will be broadcast in temperate Europe.

Common crane

Grus grus

NORTHERN EURASIA; SOME WINTER IN AFRICA, INDIA AND
SOUTHEAST ASIA, 95–120 cm (37–47 in)

 CRANES DON'T SING, BUT THEY CERTAINLY make music. They are impressive soloists, but in flocks they elevate an encounter into an experience.

A few years ago, I was visiting Berlin, Germany, on a grey autumnal day in that somewhat grey city. The centre thronged with people and traffic, with everybody going about their business, looking down. At a particular kerbside the lights turned red and, momentarily, shoppers coalesced. In the pause I unexpectedly heard what sounded like a distant bugle coming from the sky. And there, way above the buildings and the busyness of the street, was a flock of cranes in perfect V-formation, plying the skies with slow, powerful wingbeats. A few more blasts on the bugle, ululating slightly, kept the flock together as it swept effortlessly over. The lights went green and, in my heart, I walked across the road on air.

Found over many parts of the world, cranes are very large, tall birds that wander over meadows and wade in water with a grace and elegance that is all their own. They are extremely vocal, with an unusual physical adaptation. The windpipe curves and coils around the breastbone, expanding its length enormously and amplifying the calls (in the whooping crane, *Grus americana*, the windpipe is 1.5m/5ft long). If a person had a windpipe of equivalent length, they would suffocate because stale air would collect in the coils. For the crane, however, with vastly more efficient lungs, it simply broadcasts the voice over a loudspeaker.

The windpipe curves and coils around the breastbone, expanding its length enormously and amplifying the calls.

Not surprisingly, cranes make full use of their loud voices. Pairs duet as part of their courtship and mate for life, calling to each other constantly (and presumably, if they have been together for long enough, they bicker!). Unless you were aware, you would easily pass off these practised double-blasts as the call of one bird.

Delightful as these duets are, and the contact calls of migrating birds, too, the most thrilling crane noises are made at this time of the year, when the birds follow a morning and evening routine. In many parts of their wintering range, common cranes feed on fields during the day, eating, for example, potatoes in France, or cereals and acorns in Spain. At night, however, they need a safer place to roost, so they are drawn to wetlands, where they can rest with their feet in the water or settle on islands in lakes. Such refuges are necessary from ground predators; the cranes are too big to be taken by predatory birds.

In autumn and winter, this means that cranes tend to feed some distance from where they roost, and as a result they make commuting movements between the two locations at dawn and dusk. If you bear in mind that ideal wintering crane habitat is always at a premium, this means that the commutes often involve large numbers of birds, often reaching the thousands – for example, at Spain's Laguna de Gallocanta, there may be 50,000 in November or February.

Crane movements count among the world's great bird spectacles. The sight of flocks of these enormous, elegant birds describing neat lines and Vs in the sky, and then dropping slowly down, gliding on their vast wings with necks outstretched, is truly magnificent. But it is also, of course, the sounds that they make that elevate the experience beyond anything normal. If you imagine thousands of birds all using their amplified public address voices, with each note quite similar to the trumpeting of an elephant, you get some idea of the sheer din these birds make. It won't win any prizes for musical subtlety, but as a wild sound to thrill the soul, it is hard to beat.

White-rumped shama

Copsychus malabaricus

WIDESPREAD IN INDIA AND SRI LANKA, EAST TO SOUTHEAST ASIA,
INCLUDING ISLANDS, 22–27 cm (8½–10½ in)

 IMAGINE A BIRD THAT SANG AS WELL AS A nightingale but had the looks, too. Dear readers, meet the white-rumped shama, nightingale of the East. While the European bird is dull brown all over, the shama shimmers with its glossy blue-black head, body, wings and tail, plus a richly intense orange-chestnut front. It's also a very distinctive shape, with a remarkably long tail that is white underneath and graduated (increasingly narrow towards the tip). The only thing these two birds have in common is a fabulous song and a tendency to keep themselves to themselves in thick scrub.

The shama's song is melodious, rich and varied, with well-spaced verses, and it often mimics other bird species. Males vary in the quality of their output and repertoire. Females sing too, but apparently only in the presence of the male.

If there were such a thing as a representative for the Union of Shama Singers, they would probably, with heavy heart, regret the vocal prowess of their members. Because the many desirable attributes of the shama have conferred on it an unwanted status as one of the most popular cage birds in the world. Ownership is particularly popular in Southeast Asia, where the euphonious song may spill out on to the streets and add a sweetener to the din of humankind.

It cannot be denied that shamas bring great pleasure to their owners. They sing even in the small cages to which they are so often confined and don't seem to be put off by the alien environment of cities. In homes they delight owners by imitating noises, sometimes including household appliances, as well as human whistles. In many parts of Asia, people attend shama sing-offs, with prizes awarded to the winning birds. Those with the best voices – and also long tails – can command high prices among dealers. Your shama could make you rich. For example, a bird bought for a modest fee in 2021 could bring in US$80,000, if it were to win the President's Cup, a major bird-singing contest in Indonesia. Even a bird winning a lesser contest could bring its owner $20,000 in resale value. This is, of course, life-changing money.

In homes they delight owners by imitating noises, sometimes including household appliances, as well as human whistles.

There is, unfortunately, quite a different price to pay for the species as a whole. People don't only make money from showing off shamas, some also profit from catching them. In some parts of their fortunately broad range, wild shamas are being wiped out; they are, for example, becoming rare on Java and have been lost from Singapore. There is even talk of a widespread captive breeding effort to deter this illegal practice. At the moment, songbird contests are known to occur in 19 different countries and are a major driver in the cage-bird trade.

There is a curious rider to the shama's 1,000-year association with humanity, an unlikely sequence of events that have given it a strange claim to fame. It was probably the very first bird in the world to have its song recorded. (Bearing in mind that the sounds of almost every one of the planet's 11,000 bird species are now in a library, that's quite a thing.) And the recording was made by an eight-year-old boy! In 1889 Ludwig Koch was playing with an early Edison phonograph and he unknowingly recorded the song of a family pet shama. There might have been previous attempts, but this is the first known.

Ludwig Koch lived a remarkable life. He was a precocious violinist and spent his late childhood as a professional singer. During the First World War he worked for German intelligence, and later for the government. Despite the fact he was a Jew, the notorious Nazi politician and war leader Hermann Göring was an admirer. Even so, Koch fled to Britain in 1936, and went on to achieve fame as a pioneering sound recordist and naturalist, regularly appearing on TV and radio. But his recording of a family pet in his German home is what gives him and the white-rumped shama a place in cultural history.

Yellow-rumped cacique

Cacicus cela

NORTHERN SOUTH AMERICA, MAINLY AMAZONIA,
25–28 cm (9–11 in)

LET'S ALL AGREE NOW, PASSWORDS ARE A modern curse; or at least, remembering them is the curse. It's part of our frail human condition. You might think that songbirds don't have that to worry about. But you'd be wrong. At least one bird species uses them, and furthermore it needs to keep them up to date. It has plenty to think about. It's an amazing character called the yellow-rumped cacique.

You've probably seen this bird on TV or online, since it sometimes features in films about Amazonia. It lives in noisy and conspicuous colonies of grass-built nests that hang down from high tree branches, a very effective deterrent to predators. The birds, which are glossy black and brilliant yellow, attend their colonies most of the year and there can be anything up to 250 nests in a colony, although usually many less.

The various sounds that emanate from cacique colonies are great entertainment; there are mewing sounds, gurgles, wheezes and whistles, all of which are loud. Some birds are also excellent mimics. However, it is extremely difficult to describe what you're likely to hear at a given colony because, believe it or not, each colony has its own dialect.

While it is quite well known for a bird species to have a different dialect sung by males in close proximity (see white-crowned sparrow, page 56), it is very unusual for a colony to possess its own dialect, separate from the rest. In fact, male yellow-rumped caciques have a very broad repertoire and are perfectly capable of singing songs that are very much their own, unlike the sparrows. But what they must do in the breeding season is ensure that they keep on uttering the colony's signature song type. To put it another way, to be accepted as part of the colony, they must use the password.

It makes sense. Males are very territorial, but female caciques are very fickle. It's essential to ward off strangers who might steal in and copulate with any females that are on the lookout for some variety in their lives. It pays for male colony members to know instantly when an intruder is nearby, and the best way to do so is to check whether he knows the password. If he doesn't, he's evicted. We used to play the password-exclusion game at school.

As we're all aware, it's essential to keep changing passwords to keep them off the hackers' radar. Well, astonishingly, that's the case for yellow-rumped cacique colonies too. To keep the system functioning, dialects within a given colony change over time, always from year to year and sometimes part way through a season. The members must learn them, otherwise they can be evicted. It keeps the system honest.

Of course, the colony must have a changeover of individuals to prevent inbreeding, so birds will disperse. If a bird moves to a new colony, it must quickly learn the indigenous dialect and keep up with the times, but it also takes its signature dialect with it. Scientists have found that colonies that are close to each other tend to use some shared song types; the further apart they are, the greater the difference in their language.

The breeding system in yellow-rumped caciques is hierarchical, with the dominant males mating with as many females as they can. This leaves a large number of subordinate males, who are not officially allowed to 'consort' with any of the colony females. However, what they can do is attend the site all day every day to wait until a dominant male is distracted, perhaps by going off to feed. This gives the subordinate a chance to invite a female to a mating perch.

To keep the system functioning, dialects within a given colony change over time, always from year to year and sometimes part way through a season.

Some subordinates are successful. And that proves something we may have all suspected. We can't always trust our 'friends', even when they know the password.

Ring-necked dove

Streptopelia capicola

EASTERN AND SOUTHERN AFRICA, 25 cm (AROUND 10 in)

OVER THE YEARS, THERE MUST HAVE BEEN thousands of documentaries made about African wildlife. Most of them feature the great icons of the savannah – elephants, lions and giraffes. Refreshingly, less common animals such as elephant shrews and hyraxes are occasionally featured, especially these days, as well as vulture scrums and stunning, colourful birds.

However, there's one set of characters that feature on almost all of these documentaries and never get a mention – doves. They are ubiquitous in sub-Saharan Africa, yet overlooked. Sometimes they do appear on-screen, particularly at waterholes where crocodiles inevitably lie in wait for some four-legged herbivore, and they fly off at the dénouement, the splashing and death. More often, though, they feature on the soundtrack. They are the perennial extras.

This isn't a pitch to make a safari film on the lives of ring-necked doves, because they genuinely do lack charisma. What they do, though, is set the scene. The advertising calls of doves are the true voices of Africa. They are extraordinarily persistent in their vocalizations, seeming to start at the break of dawn and cease at dusk with almost no pauses, even in the heat of the day. They sometimes call in the middle of the night. They also advertise for absolutely every day of the year.

This particular species makes a sound that radiates hot, dry habitats. It is a three-note coo with emphasis on the middle syllable, making 'puk, crrrr, puk' or, with imagination, 'Ring-NECKED-dove'. This helps separate it from its equally abundant colleague the red-eyed dove (*Streptopelia semitorquata*), which gives a series of six fast coos in a phrase resembling 'Red-ed-eyed dove, I AM'. There are other doves, too, in the African bush, and these all combine coos with rolling sounds, but in different ways; it's all a little like dove Morse code.

> *The advertising calls of doves are the true voices of Africa. They are extraordinarily persistent in their vocalizations, seeming to start at the break of dawn and cease at dusk.*

All these advertising calls are hot in other ways, too. Not only do the males sing in order to keep a territory and attract a mate, but also their calls serve to keep the female 'in the mood'. The females are stimulated by hearing the male's song – more accurately, they are actually stimulated by their own vocal response to the song. When they call in reply, their ovaries begin to enlarge to prepare for breeding. Doves form strong pair bonds and these can be long-lasting, sometimes for life. The birds have a likeable habit of perching close together in body contact, not doing anything much except for waiting for the next safari crew to come along.

Incidentally, you might wonder why doves are so often featured at waterhole scenes. It is partly because they have a diet of grain, nutritious but very dry, requiring them to drink a great deal. But they also have an ability that is unusual among birds – they can suck. Most bird species practise a method called 'scoop and tilt', which means they must gather water in the bill, then lift their head to get it down the throat. Pigeons and doves will tilt their heads up while drinking, but they can take in much more water at a time.

It is the doves' party trick, shared by few birds except parrots and a few small finch-like characters. But is anybody watching?

Common myna

Acridotheres tristis

CENTRAL AND SOUTHERN ASIA; WIDELY INTRODUCED,
25–25 cm (9–10 in)

 THERE IS LITTLE DOUBT THAT MORE HUMAN ears have heard the crow of the cockerel than any other bird species – but which voluble species might be in second place? Could it be this irrepressible character, the common myna? It abounds in some of the most populous regions of the world, including India, southern China and Southeast Asia, and has been introduced to parts of Africa and Australia, as well as a multitude of islands throughout the tropics. It is completely at home everywhere, from cities to rural villages. And if it is present, then its loud, slightly cranky voice ensures you cannot fail to hear it.

You wouldn't want to play a continuous reel of common myna calls and songs to help you relax, but there's no doubt that they create an atmosphere. This bird whistles loudly, shrieks like a parrot, makes snarling and grating calls, and will even make attractive fluting noises. The song is a general combination of different calls and has been written, for example, as 'Hee-hee-chirka-chirka-chirka', which gives a good idea. It would undoubtedly take several pages of this book to go through all the renditions, so we'll take loud, piercing and squawky as a given.

For centuries, people have kept common mynas in captivity, not because they want to hear the cacophony, but because of this bird's powers of mimicry. In common with some other members of the starling family, it shows great expertise in appropriating a range of sounds, which in this case includes crying human babies, the meowing of cats, phone sounds and human speech. There are plenty of examples on YouTube.

It shows great expertise in appropriating a range of sounds, which in this case includes crying human babies, the meowing of cats, phone sounds and human speech.

Not everybody is a fan, though, and there is one habit that can test humans to the limit of their patience. If you realize that one pair of mynas are noisy and a flock of mynas are very noisy, then imagine what it must be like to hear hundreds of them, or even thousands. This is a daily reality for those who live close to a communal roost of these birds. Every evening, mynas gather from all corners and perch in a large, leafy tree, or in a building, such as a station or warehouse, and gabble. They do this for about half an hour, and during that time they sometimes fly around in impressive aerial manoeuvres. The din can be enough to hear above the roar of traffic, and in rural areas can be deafening. The birds usually go quiet for a while after sunset, but the problem is that every so often during the night, they will suddenly launch into outbreaks of communal whispering that can become very noisy before quietening down, as if a conductor has tapped a baton, all enough to awaken nearby human slumbers. One of the bird's Sanskrit names translates as 'one who is fond of arguments'; and regrettably in some places, roosts are occupied all year round.

In 2000, the common myna suddenly found itself declared 'birda' non grata, not because of its roosting habits but because of its success as an introduced species. The IUCN Species Survival Commission (SSC) placed it on a list of the world's 100 most invasive species. In a 2008 survey it was similarly reproached for being 'Australia's Most Significant Pest/Problem' and was often christened the 'flying rat'. In areas outside its natural range, the common myna can be a serious threat to indigenous species, owing to its aggressiveness, especially at potential hole-nesting sites. It also attacks crops.

These problems are expanding. In recent years the common myna has colonized Portugal, Spain, Israel and Florida, among other places, and there are signs that it could yet expand to many other parts of the world, taking its noisy voice with it. Soon, it seems, it will cement that second place as the world's most loquacious runner-up.

White-nest swiftlet

Aerodramus fuciphagus

INDONESIA AND BORNEO, 11–12 cm (AROUND 4½ in)

 AROUND THE WORLD, THE FUNCTIONS OF bird sounds are many and varied, as hopefully this yearly diary has revealed. However, one use that we haven't covered so far is echolocation – locating an object by reflected sound (see below). This is extremely rare among birds and only two types use it, both breeding in dark caves. One is a rare inhabitant of South America and the Caribbean known as the oilbird (*Steatornis caripensis*), and the others, occurring much more widely, are a group of small members of the swift family, appropriately known as swiftlets. A dozen or so species are known, mostly found in Asia. This species, the white-nest swiftlet, used to be known as the edible-nest swiftlet and its nest was the original ingredient of bird's-nest soup.

Echolocation is a form of sonar. An animal makes a noise, then measures how long it takes for the echo to return in order to locate the position of an object. Bats are the ultimate exponents of the art. They are so good that some can detect ultra-thin wire and fly around it and they can, of course, catch flying insects in complete darkness. It requires ultrasonic frequencies of very high energy to do this effectively, with peak energy at 3o–7okHz, reaching up to about 1ookHz, all of which is well out of human range.

Swiftlets don't have anything like these abilities. Their clicks are in the range of 3–1okHz and are easily audible to us. The fact that the frequencies are relatively low means that swiftlets cannot perceive much detail. However, unlike bats, they don't use their abilities to hunt and chase down food. They are day-living creatures that do all their hunting outside the caves, as any other type of swift would do. They catch flying insects using sight, only using echolocation to find their way through cave systems where they roost every night, and where they nest during the wet season.

They catch flying insects using sight, only using echolocation to find their way through cave systems where they roost every night, and where they nest during the wet season.

The low frequencies mean that swiftlets can only perceive objects 4–2omm (⅛–¾in) in diameter, with some species performing better than others. This, though, is perfectly adequate for cave navigation, where they need to avoid colliding with each other, first and foremost, and otherwise must avoid projections and rock faces. They can also, presumably, detect their own nest sites and the immediate topography of the nesting walls.

It has to be one of the mysteries of hunter-gathering history that anyone should ever have thought of trying to eat the nest of a swiftlet. Not only are they spirited away in dark caves, often high up towards the ceiling, where it is difficult not only to find them but also reach them – they are bracket-shaped and entirely self-supporting – but also they are made of nothing more than the bird's saliva. Helpfully, the birds do nest in colonies, and these days they are also often found in buildings in urban areas, but the nests have been appreciated in Chinese cuisine and medicine for centuries.

The question is, though, who tried the nest-eating stunt in the first place? It was obviously a hit, and apparently the nests are highly nutritious and have a rich, fulsome taste. Had the original discoverer still been in the business now, they would be exceedingly wealthy – 1lb (0.5kg) of dried nests can fetch up to US$10,000.

But the caves are smelly, often copiously coated with the birds' droppings, home to some of the world's leggiest invertebrates, and liable to the occasional collapse. Whoever discovered the secret must have super-powers of detection that not even the swiftlets possess.

Island canary

Serinus canaria

ATLANTIC ISLANDS OFF NORTH AFRICA,

12–13 cm (AROUND 5 in)

WHEN PEOPLE FIRST ARRIVED ON THE Atlantic islands off North Africa, now known as the Canary Islands, they couldn't possibly have known how significant the meeting of small bird and upright ape was going to be. No doubt the first people listened to the song of the native small finch, which also occurs on Madeira and the Azores, and were impressed by it. And no wonder; it is a fabulous, silvery song, a lively succession of trills, twitters, tweets and gentle buzzes, bursting with effervescence and delightfully varied. It lifts the soul.

To cut a long story short, the song was so admired that by the 16th century the canary was brought to Europe as a sweet-voiced cage bird. Thus began a long history of domestication that still continues today. The small, yellowish, streaky finch has been modified by selective breeding into many different colours, from bright yellow to pink, and often made larger-bodied. For centuries, breeders have exhibited their canaries at special shows.

The canary was, at one time, the most popular cage bird in the Western world. Its forced proximity to people, the ease with which it could be looked after and bred, and its tendency to sing in all circumstances endeared it to a broad range of people. Once kept only by the nobility, it became the cage bird of the people.

By the 16th century the canary was brought to Europe as a sweet-voiced cage bird. Thus began a long history of domestication that still continues today.

At the very beginning of the 20th century, the canary began a new career, which has become proverbial. The dangers of carbon monoxide poisoning in the mining industry had long been known; the deadly gas can be produced by machinery and explosives, or even by the oxidation of coal. It is a silent killer, undetectable to the human scent. In previous years, miners had the bright idea of bringing mice down mines; with their faster metabolism, it was thought that they would provide an early warning system if they began to show illness. Later, canaries were used instead. Birds have a much more efficient breathing system than we do, in which air is circulated one way during both inhalation and exhalation. The canary would thus be a much more sensitive barometer, as the cessation of singing would be easily noticed. Over the years, many lives have been saved by canaries. The birds were still used as recently as 1986.

The canary has also influenced humankind in a way that is still being felt today. You could say with some confidence that we owe the science of stem cell therapy to the birds. Until the 1980s, scientists assumed that all nerve cells (neurons) in the brain and elsewhere were generated at birth, and stayed the same throughout life. Then Fernando Nottebohm at Rockefeller University's Field Research Centre in Millbrook, New York, USA, started looking at the brains of canaries, and how they reacted to song. He found that bird song activated nerve cells in the brain (he called them 'song nuclei') and, remarkably, that the song nuclei got bigger in the spring. Could new brain cells be growing each season?

He managed to prove this by injecting the birds with thymidine, a chemical incorporated into newly created DNA – except that the thymidine was radioactive. Sure enough, when his team dissected the canaries after the breeding season, some of their brain neurons were radioactive, proving that they had been newly grown. Eventually, this discovery led to the revelation that humans, too, can produce new neurons in stem cells, so there is potential for growing new cells in damaged brain tissue. The possibilities for this new therapy are simply beyond exciting.

Eventually, this discovery led to the revelation that humans can produce new neurons in stem cells, so there is potential for growing new cells in damaged tissue. Already stem cell therapy is used in bone marrow transplants, and the future possibilities are simply beyond exciting. They include treatment for neurogenerative diseases such as Parkinson's and Alzheimer's and multiple sclerosis, as well as potential for healing heart damage and the ravages of diabetes. It will lead to a better world for humanity.

And that's something to sing about.

Great tit

Parus major

EURASIA AND NORTH AFRICA, 13–15 cm (5–6 in)

FOR MOST OF US, THE FEAST OF CHRISTMAS has passed, and New Year is around the corner. It would be far-fetched to suggest that our wild birds would have noticed these events, but it so happens that this time of year is crucial to them, too. The winter solstice falls on 21 or 22 December each year, coinciding with the reverse in the southern hemisphere. In the north it marks the shortest day, and in the south, the longest.

In Europe, you might have noticed that something has been happening outside. Assuming that the weather hasn't been ferocious, you might have picked up some snatches of bird song. These aren't from robins or song thrushes, which have been going for some time. These are new. They include, perhaps as their main spokes-bird, the great tit.

The great tit isn't a great songster, but its voice has an insistence and a cheer that makes it cut through the sludge of a December day and lift your heart. It is a simple repetition of 'Tea-cher' to make a short phrase: 'Tea-cher, tea-cher, tea-cher,' with many variations (to Americans, it's similar to the song of the tufted titmouse (*Baeolophus bicolor*). Although it starts in December, it will be significantly obvious in January, and incessant by February as males set up and defend territories.

These mid- and late winter whisperings are significant. Although modest now, they will be far-reaching. The stirring of songs coincides with some remarkable internal stirrings.

Many biological systems need to be regulated to the time of year. For example, it would be disastrous for a bird to breed when there isn't enough food around, or to migrate too late. So, every bird needs an internal time clock, not just for the day itself but for the season. And while the weather gives a guide to seasonal changes, we all know – and the birds 'know' – that it is fickle and unreliable. The only external cue for a wild bird living in a strongly seasonal latitude that is entirely predictable and reliable is day length (in the tropics, rains are often a cue.)

As we know, then, the days are just beginning to get longer. It might be too early for a bird to sense this, but within a few weeks it certainly will. That's because, in its brain, it has a way of measuring the change in day length.

Remarkably, the light-detecting cells are in the hypothalamus, deep inside the brain. Light does not reach it through the bird's eyes, but instead comes through the feathers, skull and surrounding tissues. Long wavelength, low frequency red light fires up photoreceptors – specialized cells that detect light. These then convey impulses through sensory neurons to the site where the brain regulates the release of hormones. And this in turn sets off a cascade of hormone chemical conversations, which switch on many different mechanisms in the body. One of these is to regrow the nascent gonads, which in most birds are switched off after the breeding season and regress to almost nothing.

And another process that is switched on is song. A major part of the hormone cascade is the production of testosterone. As it surges, the male bird sings more – it cannot help itself. The tap keeps on running as the weeks go by. Although the song output will also be modified by weather and temperature, the process is now irreversible.

Remarkably, the light-detecting cells are in the hypothalamus, deep inside the brain. Light does not reach it through the bird's eyes, but instead comes through the feathers, skull and surrounding tissues.

So, if you hear a great tit singing at this most gloomy time of year in northern Eurasia, you are hearing something of great significance. It is the very noise of the year turning, and turning in the direction that those of us up here will be pleased about.

Index

Acknowledgements

Many thanks to my commissioning editor, Tina Persaud, for getting the project underway, and to Lilly Phelan for her hard work in pulling all the strands together so efficiently. Grateful thanks, too, to Madeleine Floyd for bringing the essays to life with her wonderfully lively illustrations.

I always owe a huge debt to my family for coping with me in book writing times, especially my wife Carolyn. As to Emmie and Sam – you'll have both left home by the time this book is published, and making your own, exciting ways in life – fashion and music. I love you all.

Finally, I have been fortunate to have some fantastic mentors and colleagues, who encouraged me in various ways to pursue my love of bird song. Not all are still here, but they are in my memories. Special thanks to Ron Kettle, Jeffery Boswall, Jim Gulledge, Pat Sellar, Richard Ranft, Nigel Bewley and John Wyatt.

We would like to thank xeno-canto (xeno-canto.org) for providing an open platform for sharing sound recordings of nature, and the following recordists for their contribution:

James Lidster (526700, 528403), Simon Elliott (670607, 585770, 660388, 590432, 595646, 592609, 599064, 593412), Ted Floyd (589306, 171727, 368388), Geoffrey Monchaux (455189), Susanne Kuijpers (632170, 662788, 630117, 639563, 650636, 662356, 642477), Richard Webster (188828, 575058, 629330, 504149), Annette Hamann (358722), Hazel Reeves (658286), Andrew Spencer (33467, 33594, 122325, 22414, 72499, 547500), David Darrell-Lambert (476931), Peter Boesman (472721, 472767, 369104, 369018, 359519, 374956), Gabriel Leite (420914, 591731), David La Puma (364466), Frank Lambert (409007 182994), James Ray (570705), Tim Cockcroft (662581, 411728), Mike Fitzgerald (488177), Greg Mclachlan (357317), Samuel Levy (626027), Javier Garcia Saez (698384).

All recordings included in this book can be heard at www.batsfordbooks.com/a-year-of-songbirds/ and xeno-canto.org

Further reading

Birds of the World (Cornell Lab of Ornithology) – birdsoftheworld.org

Donald Kroodsma, *Listening to a Continent Sing* (Princeton University Press, 2016)

Donald Kroodsma, *The Singing Life of Birds*, Houghton Mifflin (Harcourt, 2005)

Handbook of the Birds of the World - Volume 16 (Lynx Edicions, 2011)

Irby J. Lovette and John W. Fitzpatrick (ed.) *The Cornell Lab of Ornithology Handbook of Bird Biology* (Wiley, 2016)

Joel Carl Welty and Luis Baptista, *The Life of Birds* (Saunders Publishing, 1988)

Mark Cocker and Richard Mabey, *Birds Britannica* (Chatto & Windus, 2005)

Mark Cocker, *Birds and People* (Jonathan Cape, 2013)

Tim Low, *Where Song Began* (Penguin, 2014)